Contexts in Literature

# Metaphysical Poetry

Richard Willmott

Series editor: Adrian Barlow

CAMBRIDGE
UNIVERSITY PRESS

CAMBRIDGE UNIVERSITY PRESS
Cambridge, New York, Melbourne, Madrid, Cape Town, Singapore,
São Paulo, Delhi, Dubai, Tokyo

Cambridge University Press
The Edinburgh Building, Cambridge CB2 8RU, UK

www.cambridge.org
Information on this title: www.cambridge.org/9780521789608

First published 2002
Reprinted 2005, 2008

*A catalogue record for this publication is available from the British Library*

ISBN 978-0-521-78960-8 Paperback

Transferred to digital printing 2009

Prepared for publication by Gill Stacey
Designed by Tattersall Hammarling & Silk
Cover illustration: Henry Vaughan's Poems *Silex Scintillans* by courtesy of
The British Library

# Contents

# Introduction

It was at a time of political turbulence, new ideas and exciting discoveries in the late 16th and 17th centuries that the poetry we now call metaphysical came to be written. Its emotional power and intellectual challenge are such that it still appeals to modern readers in its own right, while also opening up an understanding of the times and culture in which it was written and from which our own culture has developed. This book aims to point the way to exploring the poetry by providing an introduction to its cultural and historical context. It also looks at some of the many ways in which readers at different times have read the poetry, suggesting approaches for readers today.

## What is metaphysical poetry?

The question 'What is metaphysical poetry?' demands attention, but is difficult to answer. To say that it is poetry of the late 16th and 17th centuries 'characterised by subtlety of thought and complex imagery' *(Concise Oxford Dictionary)* points in the right direction, but is too general to be very helpful. However, a more precise definition would be misleadingly restrictive, because the term 'metaphysical' can be used to describe a wide range of poetry. Nevertheless, there are certain typical characteristics that *can* be identified as metaphysical. Foremost of these is the ingenuity with which the poets use language and ideas, often making startling comparisons of apparently unlike objects which are then worked out in considerable detail. John Donne's famous comparison of the twin arms of a pair of compasses to a pair of lovers in 'A Valediction: Forbidding Mourning' is one of the most extreme examples of this type of comparison known as a metaphysical conceit.

Other characteristics of metaphysical poetry include its range of reference, for example to religious and political controversies and to new scientific and geographical discoveries. Sometimes these topics are considered in their own right; sometimes they are used to provide comparisons to illustrate other concerns. Typically, metaphysical poets are very involved in what they are writing about. They write with highly individual voices and often with a sense of drama. Consequently when they present their reasoned (or apparently reasoned) arguments, they do so with emotion as well as intellectual subtlety, and often make use of paradox and irony. In some of the poets (Donne in particular), the personal voice is also heard in a deliberate irregularity of rhythm, but metaphysical versification ranges from the deliberately rough to the smoothly musical.

# Who were the metaphysical poets?

As you read the metaphysicals, you will see how this very general description needs to be filled out in much greater detail, but you will also come to recognise the sheer variety of metaphysical style. There are, for example, considerable differences between the earliest poems of John Donne (1572–1633) and the later poems of Andrew Marvell (1621–1678), although both these poets are commonly labelled metaphysical. On the other hand, there are often similarities between the poems of Donne and his exact contemporary, Ben Jonson, although the latter is not considered a metaphysical poet. This example provides a warning that although the term 'metaphysical poetry' points to an important aspect of poetry in the late 16th century and much of the 17th century, it is not one that can be too tightly defined in terms of either style or practitioners.

Nevertheless, it will be helpful to know that the poets referred to most frequently in this book are John Donne, George Herbert, Richard Crashaw, Henry Vaughan and Andrew Marvell, together with Katherine Philips who, although not normally thought of as a metaphysical, at times makes something new of metaphysical imagery and ideas. Cross reference has been made to various minor metaphysical poets and a number of 'non-metaphysical' poets including Ben Jonson, Aemilia Lanyer, Mary Wroth and Robert Herrick, and also to translations of earlier works made during this period.

# How this book is organised

## Chronology

The chronology lists some of the major events, public and private, that influenced the poets' writing.

## Part 1: The historical and cultural background

Part 1 gives brief biographies of the major metaphysical poets' lives and then offers introductions to:

- the rediscovery of classical culture and learning known as the Renaissance

- some of the key Christian ideas that influenced the poets and which were the subject of argument in the Reformation and Counter Reformation

- some of the major historical events of the 16th and 17th centuries that affected the lives of the poets.

## Part 2: Approaching the poems

Part 2 examines some of the different types of poetry written by the metaphysical poets.

## Part 3: Texts and extracts

This part contains poems and extracts discussed in the rest of the book, or used as a focus for tasks and assignments.

## Part 4: Critical approaches to the poetry

Part 4 summarises the ways in which critics and readers have approached metaphysical poetry, both in the past and more recently.

## Part 5: How to write about metaphysical poetry

Part 5 offers guidelines and assignments for students covering this topic as part of an advanced course in literary studies.

## Part 6: Resources

This final part contains suggestions for further reading and research, a glossary and an index.

Terms that appear in the glossary are highlighted in bold when they first appear in the main text.

Throughout this book and at the ends of Parts 1, 2, 4 and 5 there are tasks and assignments designed to address the issues raised in the text.

# Chronology

| | |
|---|---|
| **1534** | Act of Supremacy declares Henry VIII Supreme Head of English Church |
| **1535** | Execution of Sir Thomas More |
| **1546** | Death of German religious reformer, Martin Luther |
| **1547** | Death of Henry VIII; accession of Edward VI |
| **1553** | Death of Edward VI; accession of Queen Mary and restoration of Catholicism |
| **1558** | Death of Mary; accession of Elizabeth I and restoration of Protestant Church of England |
| **1562** | Council of Trent calls for militant opposition to heretics (i.e. non-Catholics) |
| **1564** | Shakespeare, Marlowe and Galileo born; Michelangelo and Calvin die |
| **1569** | Mercator's Map of the World |
| **1570** | Pope excommunicates Elizabeth I |
| **1572** | John Donne and Ben Jonson born; Massacre of St Bartholomew (Protestants massacred in Paris) |
| **1577–1580** | Drake circumnavigates the world |
| **1584** | Raleigh discovers Virginia |
| **1588** | Armada defeated |
| **1591** | Robert Herrick born |
| **1592** | Donne admitted to Lincoln's Inn |
| **1593** | George Herbert born; Mary Sidney working on translation of Psalms started by her brother Philip (died 1586) |
| **1595** | Robert Southwell, poet and Jesuit priest, executed at Tyburn |
| **1596** | Donne takes part in sack of Cadiz under Earl of Essex |
| **1601** | Donne MP for Brackley; secretly marries Anne More |
| **1603** | Elizabeth I dies; accession of James VI of Scotland as James I of England |
| **1605** | Gunpowder plot: Catholics fail to blow up Houses of Parliament |
| **1609** | Herbert goes up to Trinity College, Cambridge |
| **1611** | Authorised Version (King James Bible) published; Aemilia Lanyer's *Salve Deus Rex Iudaeorum* published |
| **1612** | Richard Crashaw born |
| **1615** | Donne ordained priest |
| **1616** | Shakespeare dies; Jonson's *Works* (1st Folio) published |
| **1617** | Anne Donne dies |
| **1618** | Abraham Cowley born |
| **1620** | Herbert appointed Public Orator at Cambridge; Pilgrim Fathers sail to North America |

| | |
|---|---|
| **1621** | Donne appointed Dean of St Paul's; Andrew Marvell born; Henry Vaughan and his twin Thomas born; Mary Wroth's *Pamphilia to Amphilanthus* published |
| **1624** | Herbert MP for Montgomery |
| **1625** | Death of James I and VI; accession of Charles I |
| **1628** | William Harvey publishes *De Motu Cordis* on the circulation of blood |
| **1630** | Herbert ordained priest and becomes rector of Bemerton |
| **1631** | Donne preaches 'Death's Duel'; dies 31 March; Dryden born |
| **1633** | First edition of Donne's poems; Herbert dies and *The Temple* published posthumously; Galileo forced by Roman Catholic Church to retract claim that the earth goes round the sun; William Laud appointed Archbishop of Canterbury |
| **1637** | Thomas Traherne born |
| **1640** | Jonson's *Works* (2nd Folio) published |
| **1642** | Start of Civil Wars; Battle of Edgehill; theatres in London closed |
| **1644** | Battle of Marston Moor; celebration of Christmas forbidden |
| **1645** | Cromwell wins Battle of Naseby; Archbishop Laud executed; use of *Book of Common Prayer* forbidden |
| **1646** | Charles I surrenders to Scots; Crashaw's *Steps to the Temple* and Vaughan's *Poems with the Tenth Satire of Juvenal Englished* published |
| **1648** | Herrick's *Hesperides* published; Parliament 'purged' |
| **1649** | Charles I executed; Declaration of the Commonwealth; Crashaw dies |
| **1650** | Cromwell reconquers Ireland; Marvell writes 'An Horatian Ode upon Cromwell's Return from Ireland'; first part of Vaughan's *Silex Scintillans* published |
| **1652** | Crashaw's *Carmen Deo Nostro* published |
| **1655** | Vaughan's *Silex Scintillans* published with second part |
| **1656** | Cowley's *Works* published |
| **1657** | Marvell appointed as assistant Latin secretary to Milton |
| **1658** | Death of Oliver Cromwell |
| **1659** | Marvell elected MP for Hull |
| **1660** | Restoration of Charles II |
| **1662** | *Book of Common Prayer* reissued |
| **1664** | War with Dutch starts; unauthorised edition of Katherine Philips's *Poems*; Katherine Philips dies |
| **1667** | Successful Dutch raid on Chatham harbour; peace signed with Dutch; Marvell writes 'The Last Instructions to a Painter'; first edition of Milton's *Paradise Lost* published; Cowley dies |
| **1674** | Traherne dies (most of his poetry unpublished until 20th century) |
| **1678** | Marvell dies |
| **1681** | Marvell's *Miscellaneous Poems* published |
| **1695** | Vaughan dies |

# The historical and cultural background

- Who were the metaphysical poets?

- How does metaphysical poetry fit into the life of 17th-century England?

- How important were religion and science to the metaphysical poets?

Part 1 looks at the ways in which the Renaissance, religious controversy, political conflict and contemporary culture influenced the writing of metaphysical poetry.

## Brief lives of some metaphysical poets

### John Donne (1572–1631)

The writer of racy, sexually explicit poetry and of powerful religious verse, John Donne was born into a committed Roman Catholic family. He was related through his mother to Sir Thomas More, who had been executed for refusing to take the oath of supremacy acknowledging Henry VIII as head of the Church of England (see page 21). His great-uncle, Thomas Heywood, a former monk, had been executed for his Catholic faith in 1574 and his uncle, Jasper Heywood, had given up a promising career at Oxford to become leader of the **Jesuit** mission in England and had been arrested trying to flee the country.

The details of Donne's education are not entirely clear. He went to Oxford in 1584 at the age of 12 (at the age of 16 all students were required to subscribe to the 'Thirty Nine Articles' – the Church of England's summary of religious doctrine – and to avoid doing this, Catholic children often went to university at a very young age). He may have then studied at Cambridge and spent some time abroad, but in 1592 it is known that he joined Lincoln's Inn, one of the Inns of Court. The Inns of Court in London were (and still are) the collegiate institutions from which lawyers conducted their business and where those who wished to join the profession received their training. In Elizabethan times, they were both something like a third university in addition to Oxford and Cambridge and at the same time a place where young men from good families – and often with no intention of studying the law – could meet others of their own class and enjoy themselves, while being part of a cultured and politically aware society. It was as such a young man about town (although outside court circles himself) that Donne wrote his *Satires,* revealing both how he was attracted to fashionable court life and how aware he was of the pretence and sham that lay behind many people's attempts to be noticed there.

However, in 1593, at about the time that Donne was writing the earliest of his *Satires*, his younger brother, Henry, was arrested for sheltering a Jesuit priest and sent to Newgate prison. Henry died of the plague before being brought to trial. Clearly if Donne was to achieve his ambition of having a successful political career in Protestant England, he had to reconsider his faith. It seems reasonable to assume that he had made, or was close to making, the decision to abandon his Catholic faith when, in 1596, he took part in the destruction of part of Catholic Spain's fleet and the sack of Cadiz under the Earl of Essex, and then in the relatively unsuccessful raid on the Azores in 1597.

One of Donne's companions on the expedition to the Azores was the son of Sir Thomas Egerton, Lord Keeper of the Great Seal and an important political figure. Shortly afterwards Donne was employed as Sir Thomas's secretary and in 1601 he became Member of Parliament for Brackley in Northamptonshire, a seat which was under the control of Egerton. Since political power was centred on the royal Court, MPs had very little influence, but even so this was a further step towards the political success that he desired. However, towards the end of 1601 Donne secretly married Anne More, niece of Egerton's second wife, who was living in the house under his protection. When the truth was discovered Egerton sacked Donne, and Sir George More, his new father-in-law, had him imprisoned. Although he was released in due course, his hopes of a political career were finished: 'John Donne, Ann Donne, Un-done,' as he is supposed to have punned in a letter to his wife at the time.

In the period between Donne's marriage and his ordination as a priest in the Church of England, he lived in relative poverty. In 1615 he abandoned his hopes of employment at Court and was ordained. Donne had not completely abandoned ambition, however, since he made sure before his ordination that he would be given employment. In fact, King James appointed him a chaplain and obliged the unwilling University of Cambridge to make him a Doctor of Divinity. A year later he was appointed Divinity Reader at Lincoln's Inn, and then in 1621, Dean of St Paul's Cathedral in London. Although Donne's decision to enter the Church gave him both status and an audience (he preached before the king as well as in the cathedral and Lincoln's Inn), it should not be thought of solely as a shrewd career move: the sense of unworthiness revealed in his poetry and the urgency of his preaching suggest how important Donne's religious faith was to him.

In 1631 Donne died, having preached his last sermon before the Court. This sermon was published posthumously as *Death's Duel,* and two years later his poems were also published posthumously.

## George Herbert (1593–1633)

Unlike Donne, George Herbert came from a strongly Protestant family. He was a distant relative of one of the leading Protestant members of Court, William Herbert,

Earl of Pembroke, and therefore well placed to receive exactly the sort of patronage and promotion for which Donne was so desperate. Certainly the early stages of his career were rapid. He was educated first at Westminster School and in 1609 he went up to Trinity College, Cambridge. By 1620 he was Public Orator at Cambridge, a position from which two of his predecessors had become Secretaries of State and in which he attracted King James's praise as being the 'Jewel' of the university.

One reason that Donne had been reluctant to be ordained was what he called the 'Lay-scornings of the Ministry', in other words the low opinion that many people had of ministers or priests. It seems clear that Herbert too may have had some reservations about depressing his social status by becoming ordained, as is suggested in lines 9–12 from 'The Quip' (the third line in this extract refers to the fact that Herbert was a keen amateur musician):

> Then Money came, and chinking still,
> 'What tune is this, poor man?' said he.
> 'I heard in music you had skill.'
> But thou shalt answer, Lord, for me.

Nevertheless, it is also clear that Herbert took his Christian faith very seriously long before he gave up hope of political advancement. In 1624 he became MP for Montgomery, a seat that was under the control of his kinsman, the Earl of Pembroke, but towards the end of that year he gained dispensation from the Archbishop to be ordained deacon without the normal one year delay. (A deacon is a minister in the third rank of the clergy below bishops and priests.) What triggered the apparent suddenness of this decision is not clear. It may have been because he was aware that political advancement was increasingly unlikely, but also because he felt that it was his vocation to be a clergyman. He may not have immediately given up hope of worldly advancement, but in 1630 he took the next step of being ordained a priest and became rector of Bemerton. This was a small parish where the clergyman was appointed by the Earl of Pembroke and was close to the latter's great house at Wilton, just outside Salisbury.

Herbert looked after his small parish conscientiously and also enjoyed making music. He died in 1633, having entrusted his poems to his friend Nicholas Ferrar for publication – they were published later that same year.

## Richard Crashaw (1612/13–1649)

Ironically Richard Crashaw, the most extravagantly **baroque** of the metaphysical poets, and in later life a convert to Roman Catholicism, was the son of a **Puritan** clergyman. He was educated at Charterhouse and then at Pembroke Hall, Cambridge. In 1635 he became a fellow of Peterhouse, the Cambridge college that supported most enthusiastically the emphasis on ceremonial worship that Archbishop Laud was imposing on the Church of England (see pages 25–26). Crashaw was ordained a priest in 1638 and became curate of the church of Little St Mary's next to Peterhouse.

He appears to have left Cambridge before Puritan reformers smashed the stained glass windows and pulled down the statues in Peterhouse chapel and Little St Mary's in 1643, although it was not until the following year that he was officially ejected from his fellowship. He then fled to the Continent and converted to Roman Catholicism (although the majority of his poetry was written while he was still a member of the Church of England). It was while he was living in poverty in Paris that the poet Cowley apparently introduced him to Charles I's queen, Henrietta Maria – who was a Catholic – in the hope of finding him some patronage. Crashaw died a few years later, a sub-canon (minor clerical official) at the shrine of Loreto in Italy. Cowley's poem 'On the Death of Mr Richard Crashaw' gives a tolerant and affectionate picture of his character. This extract is from lines 37–58:

> How well, blest swan [i.e. Crashaw], did Fate contrive thy death,
> And made thee render up thy tuneful breath
> In thy great mistress' arms! Thou most divine
> And richest offering of Loreto's shrine!
> ...
> Angels, they say, brought the famed chapel there,
> And bore the sacred load in triumph through the air.
> 'Tis surer much they brought thee there, and they,
> And thou, their charge, went singing all the way.
> Pardon, my mother Church, if I consent
> That angels led him when from thee he went;
> For even in error sure no danger is
> When joined with so much piety as his.
> Ah, mighty God, with shame I speak it, and grief,
> Ah, that our greatest faults were in belief!
> And our weak reason were even weaker yet,
> Rather than thus our wills too strong for it.
> His faith, perhaps, in some nice tenents might
> Be wrong; his life, I'm sure, was in the right.
> And I myself a Catholic will be,
> So far, at least, great saint, to pray to thee.

**mother Church**  Cowley belonged to the Church of England
**Angels ... famed chapel there**  the home of the Virgin Mary was allegedly
    carried to Loreto by angels
**tenents**  subtly defined articles of belief

## Andrew Marvell (1621–1678)

Andrew Marvell, the son of another Puritan clergyman, was educated at Hull Grammar School and went up to Trinity College, Cambridge in 1633. In 1639 it seems that he briefly converted to Roman Catholicism and ran away to London, but his father found him and sent him back to Cambridge. Unlike Crashaw, Marvell subsequently remained firmly Protestant in his convictions.

Nevertheless, he avoided involvement in the Civil Wars, travelling on the Continent between 1642 and 1647, before being employed by the retired parliamentary general, Lord Fairfax, as tutor to his daughter, Mary. Then from 1653 he was tutor to William Dutton – a private post, but one with public links since at the time Dutton was expected to marry Oliver Cromwell's daughter.

In 1657 Marvell was appointed as Latin Secretary to the Council of State, working alongside John Milton on the drafting and translating of documents to do with foreign affairs. The following year, Cromwell died and his son Richard summoned a new Parliament. Marvell was elected to this Parliament as one of the two MPs for Hull. Apart from a brief interruption during the manoeuvres that led to the Restoration of Charles II, he remained an MP until his death in 1678.

During the Restoration, Marvell's role in Parliament was something like that of an opposition MP today. He also wrote some satires dealing with political issues, but these poems were anonymous to protect his personal safety. Towards the end of his life, he chose to write in prose. His commitment to freedom remained as strong as ever in his last work, *An Account of the Growth of Popery and Arbitrary Government,* published anonymously in 1677, the year before his death.

It is impossible to date the majority of Marvell's poems, which, with the exception of the satires, were published after his death by his landlady, Mary Palmer, who claimed to be his wife.

## Henry Vaughan (1621–1695)

Henry Vaughan probably studied for a year or two at Jesus College, Oxford when his twin brother was there, but if so he left before taking a degree. In 1640 he went to London to study law. In 1642 he returned to his home county of Breconshire in Wales to act as a secretary to a local judge. Subsequently, he appears to have joined a Royalist troop of soldiers raised by a Colonel Price and was on the losing side in the Royalist defeat at Rowton Heath near Chester.

After his brief period of military service, Vaughan returned home, married, published his first volume of poetry in 1646 and at some point started to practise medicine. His attitude to religion was then changed by a deep religious experience that led to the writing of the poems in the two parts of *Silex Scintillans.* The distress caused by the death of his younger brother, William, in 1648 may have triggered this religious experience. The other important family influence on his life was his twin brother, Thomas, who was an alchemist and hermetical philosopher (see pages 33–34).

## Katherine Philips (1632–1664)

Katherine Philips provides yet another example of a writer turning against her upbringing. She came from a Puritan family, and her uncle was John Oxenbridge, the Puritan clergyman whose flight from persecution to Bermuda inspired Marvell's poem 'Bermudas'. Yet she became a Royalist sympathiser. When a poem expressing sympathy for Charles I was discovered by a political rival of her Parliamentarian husband, it caused him some embarrassment. At the Restoration, however, her Royalist contacts proved useful in defending him from possible prosecution.

At the age of eight, Katherine Fowler (her maiden name) had been sent to a girls' boarding school in Hackney run by a Mrs Salmon, a woman of Puritan religious convictions. Nevertheless, it was here that Katherine made some of the friendships that would draw her into Royalist circles. It was probably also here, in an all-female environment and protected from male disapproval, that she started to write poetry.

In 1646 her widowed mother married a Welsh baronet and two years later Katherine married James Philips, a distant relative of her stepfather, a supporter of Cromwell and 38 years older than she was.

Living in Wales and only occasionally visiting London, Philips created a 'Society of Friendship', a circle of friends, mainly women, whose shared ideals were inspired by her poems and letters. Members took names from pastoral plays, suggesting a desire to create an alternative world, away from the pressures of political conflicts. Katherine was 'Orinda' and two of her closest friends were 'Rosania' (Mary Aubrey) and 'Lucasia' (Anne Owen).

Although by no means all of Philips's poems of friendship are metaphysical in style, a number involve a reworking of the language and **conceits** of Donne's love poems and are of interest both in their own right and in offering a commentary on Donne. Some of the poems must have already been in circulation in manuscript when Vaughan wrote a poem praising them in 1651. However, the only edition published in her lifetime was an unauthorised one which appeared in 1664, and which was suppressed at her request (see page 25). Shortly afterwards, she died of smallpox while on a visit to London.

## The Renaissance

The period of nearly 100 years from about 1590 during which metaphysical poetry was being written was one of significant change in virtually every area of English life. The centre of political power moved from the royal Court to Parliament. The enclosure of common land and colonisation were just two elements in a changing economic situation. The final stages of the Reformation of the Church were being fought out. Scientific understanding and method were changing as well. There was a shift in emphasis from the acceptance of received knowledge to observation and analysis, whether of the movement of the planets or of the circulation of the blood. Preceding all of these changes, and contributing to them, was the gradual change across Europe in ways of thinking about literature, art and scholarship that came to be known as the Renaissance.

Renaissance literally means rebirth and refers to a new interest in the classical literature and learning of the ancient Greeks and Romans. Not all knowledge of classical writers had been lost in the Middle Ages, as is clear, for example, from the many references to writers such as Aristotle and Seneca in Chaucer (c 1343–1400), but the Renaissance saw new editions of the major authors and, in particular, the recovery in western Europe of the knowledge of Greek. In classical texts could be found everything from the hydraulics of Archimedes and advice on farming, to guidance on military tactics and on how to face life's misfortunes with dignity.

The metaphysical poets were particularly influenced by the ideas and literary styles and forms of the period around the establishment of the Roman Empire in 31 BCE (Before the Christian Era) when Octavian, later known as Augustus, defeated Mark Anthony (see page 38). Recovery of the knowledge of Greek enabled fresh study of the New Testament in its original language, rather than in the late 4th-century Latin translation prepared by St Jerome and known as the Vulgate. Ideas developed from the works of the Greek philosopher, Plato (died 347 BCE), were also widespread.

The Renaissance was a gradual process. It began in Italy and then spread to France and is generally thought of as taking place between the 14th and 16th centuries. It is generally agreed, however, that the process began later in Britain and continued through the first half of the 17th century. *– By some – Generally*
*Donne is either just beyond or on the late end of the Renaissance.*

## Translation of original texts *English Renaissance generally AFTER Italy*

A key part of the Renaissance was the discovery, editing and publishing of original texts. Thanks to the development of printing these texts became widely available. Those that were in Latin would then have been accessible to all educated people throughout western Europe, because the teaching of Latin was the starting point of all schooling. It was the standard language of scholarly debate and also the language of international diplomacy; for example the poets Milton and Marvell were both employed under Cromwell in the 1650s to write diplomatic documents in Latin, and both, like several other poets of the period, wrote Latin as well as English poetry. Nevertheless, for classical literature to exert a full influence on Renaissance literature in the different languages of Europe, it was necessary for the language gap to be crossed and this happened as large numbers of translations were produced and published. Translation in turn led to imitation, renewing the desire to rival the great classical writers.

The major themes for poetry such as love, war and the corruptions and attractions of court life existed before the Renaissance, but the Renaissance strongly influenced attitudes to them. It also provided poetic forms in which to write about such themes and had a powerful effect on the stylistic details of that writing, since style cannot be separated from subject matter and verse form. (A discussion of some of these forms comes at the end of Part 1 on pages 35–38.)

## The Reformation

Just as the Renaissance opened up an understanding of Greek and Roman civilisation, so the revival of the knowledge of Greek was a factor in the reform of the Church. This was because Greek is the original language of the New Testament (that part of the Bible added by Christian writers) and the reformers were able to justify their reforms by reference to the earliest versions of the New Testament and its description of the practice and beliefs of the early Christian Church.

Although many of the disputes of the Reformation were about organisation, authority and worship (as well as accusations of laxness, corruption and the abuse of power), at the root of the disagreements were matters of religious belief. Nor were these issues simply academic: at the time of the Reformation almost everyone in western Europe was sure that they personally were involved in God's plan for the whole of mankind. Although some had reservations about the workings of the Church, they had no doubt that at the Day of Judgement they would appear before God's throne to be set amongst either the saved or the damned. This was reflected in an enormous outpouring of poetry, written with a depth of feeling and received with a devout interest that are hard to imagine today. To understand this poetry, it is necessary to have some idea of contemporary religious ideas and controversies. To begin it will be helpful to list a number of key Christian beliefs, some of which became the subject of dispute.

- God is one, but his nature is threefold (the Trinity): God the Father, God the Son (Jesus Christ) and God the Holy Spirit (or Holy Ghost).

- God the Father created the world and the first humans, Adam and Eve.

- Eve persuaded Adam to join her in disobeying God by eating fruit from the tree of knowledge of good and evil (the Fall), and since then all humanity has been born sinful, sharing the fallen nature of Adam and Eve (original sin); see *Genesis* 1–3.

- The introduction of sin into the world brought with it death, but God in his mercy sent his Son, Jesus, to die for all people, thus rescuing them from endless sufferings in the eternal damnation of Hell and making possible their resurrection into a new spiritual life in union with God.

- This saving death of sacrifice was explained by Jesus at the Last Supper, the final meal he shared with his followers just before he was arrested by Roman soldiers. During the Last Supper he blessed and broke bread and distributed it to his disciples, telling them that it was his body which was given for them (i.e. in death on the cross) and that they should eat it. Similarly, he blessed wine and told them to drink it as his blood, given for them. He told them to do this as a memorial of him (see *I Corinthians* 11, 23–27).

- The first Christians then abandoned the Jewish custom of offering animal sacrifices as a means of being reconciled with God after having disobeyed him. Sacrifices were replaced with the service of the Mass (also referred to as Holy Communion, Eucharist or Lord's Supper in different Christian traditions). In this service the priest re-enacted the blessing and distribution of bread and wine. Although the bread and wine did not change in their visible form, it was believed that they became the body and blood of Christ when the priest consecrated (blessed) them; this is the doctrine of transubstantiation.

- Jesus was crucified on the day now commemorated on Good Friday, but on the third day he rose from the dead, commemorated on Easter Sunday, thus triumphing over death. For a further 40 days he gave final instructions to his followers. He promised that after he left them, the Holy Spirit would come to them to inspire and guide them. He then returned into union with God, commemorated on Ascension Day.

- The coming of the Holy Spirit, commemorated on Pentecost or Whit Sunday, marked the beginning of the Christian Church under the leadership of St Peter.

## The beliefs of the reformers

Since Christianity is about the salvation, or saving, of humanity from the consequences of sin, it is not surprising that two of the key issues under debate during the Reformation and the Roman Catholic Counter Reformation were the way in which people came to salvation and who was to be saved. Martin Luther (1483–1546), a German monk who became the first great leader of the Reformation, had been troubled by a strong sense of his sinfulness and a conviction that he could never hope to be saved on the basis of his good works alone, as the Catholic Church appeared to teach. He was comforted, however, when he came to the conclusion that no-one could expect to be saved on the merit of their good works and that what was required was faith alone. This faith was not simply an intellectual belief that Jesus died on the cross to save sinners, but a committed trust in God's grace – a gift that cannot be earned – and saving power. This belief – that faith was all important and that good works and gifts to the Church could not buy salvation – was a key issue that separated the reformers from the Catholic Church.

## Predestination and free will

Since, according to the reformers, salvation was dependent on God's grace, the question then arose as to whether humans were even capable of asking God for grace or whether, as many reformers believed, they were dependent on God to take the initiative and give them the grace to ask for grace. A further question was whether, since God knows everything that will happen, his foreknowledge of what humans will do means that a person has no free will, but is **predestined** to either salvation or damnation. This was the belief of the reformer, John Calvin (1509–1564), and of many, but not all, Protestants. In one of his sermons, Donne says that God 'sees all things, and foresees them, but yet this is no cause of them'. (For a study of Donne's response to the fear of damnation see pages 52–53 and the discussion of 'Batter my Heart' on pages 39–41.)

## The Psalms

An important element of worship in the reformed Churches was the singing of metrical psalms, in other words psalms arranged into metrically regular verses so that each verse could be sung to the same tune like a hymn. The Psalms are a series of 150 poems or songs traditionally attributed to King David in the Old Testament. They deal with the relationship of God and man in times of both joy and distress. However, it was not until Mary Sidney, Countess of Pembroke, took up the work started by her brother, Sir Philip Sidney, in the 1580s that a full verse translation of all 150 psalms into English was produced that had genuine literary quality. Their importance was not only in revealing the poetic quality of the Psalms in an extraordinarily wide variety of metrical forms, but in providing a model for the expression of the personal relationship between a poet and God.

▶ Read Philip Sidney's translation of 'Psalm 13' and Herbert's 'Denial' (Part 3, page 92 and page 77). Compare the ways in which frustration at the lack of a response from God, and then reconciliation with God – or at least a hint of it – are expressed. Do you find any similarities between these poems and Herbert's 'The Collar' (Part 3, page 76)?

# Political and religious change in the 17th century

The period during which metaphysical poetry was being written was one in which enormous political changes occurred including:

- the death of Elizabeth I in 1603 and the start of the Stuart dynasty when James VI of Scotland became James I of England
- the Civil Wars (1642–1648) which led to the execution of Charles I in 1649 and the establishment of the **Commonwealth** under Oliver Cromwell
- the Restoration of the monarchy with the return of Charles II in 1660.

Throughout this time of political upheaval, religion was both a cause of conflict and used to justify conflicts that had their roots in other social and economic issues. Consequently, this brief survey of public affairs will focus particularly on religious controversy.

## Church Reformation under the Tudors

The Reformation in England began in 1531 when Henry VIII (reigned 1509–1547) claimed to be supreme head of the Church in England. His decision to break with the Roman Catholic Church was not related to matters of belief. It arose rather from Henry's desire for a male heir: his marriage to Catherine of Aragon had failed to produce a male child, and Henry wished to be free to marry a wife who might bear him a son. The Pope refused to agree to his divorcing Catherine. Henry dissolved the monasteries and confiscated their lands, which he sold to the nobility and gentry, thus giving the purchasers a powerful reason to support the Reformation and to oppose any return to papal authority. Marvell's 'Upon Appleton House', written over a hundred years later, shows how the confiscations were seen and justified by those whose families had benefited from them. These extracts are from lines 217–218, 273–276 and 279–280:

> But sure those buildings last not long,
> Founded by folly, kept by wrong.
> ...
> At the demolishing, this seat
> To Fairfax fell as by escheat.
> And what both nuns and founders willed
> 'Tis likely better thus fulfilled
> ...
> Though many a nun there made her vow,
> 'Twas no religious house till now.

**seat** property
**escheat** reversion of property to a lord

The English Church began to establish its particular identity under Edward VI (1547–1553), but there was a break in the process of reform under Mary

(1553–1558), who forced the Church to turn back to Roman Catholicism. During her reign, about 300 Protestants were burned at the stake, including Cranmer, the Archbishop of Canterbury who had taken the lead in writing the first prayer book in English, *The Book of Common Prayer.*

Under Elizabeth I (reigned 1558–1603) the Church was definitely **Calvinist** in its beliefs, but its worship and system of government retained features that the Puritans regarded as Roman Catholic. Despite these disagreements the national Church remained united during Elizabeth's reign.

Because God was a higher authority than kings or queens, it was important to rulers that all their subjects recognised that they ruled by divine authority. It was the need for this alignment of allegiance to God and allegiance to the monarch that made the Pope's excommunication of Elizabeth in 1570 so important. By formally casting her out of the Roman Catholic Church and thus releasing the English from their allegiance to her, he was paving the way for any Roman Catholic to assassinate the queen in the name of a higher authority – and without fear of sin.

It was therefore a time when to be a Catholic was to be under suspicion of potential treachery and in constant fear of persecution. John Donne, born into a Catholic family was, as he put it, brought up among 'men of a suppressed and afflicted Religion'. Donne's eventual decision to abandon his Roman Catholic faith and join the Church of England was not, however, simply a matter of calculated self-interest (he had no hope of gaining political advancement as a Roman Catholic), nor can it only have been an intellectual decision. It is clear from his writings, that this was also a deeply emotional decision, which affected his feelings towards his family, but above all towards God (Satire 3, lines 93–95):

> Fool and wretch, wilt thou let thy soul be tied
> To man's laws, by which she shall not be tried
> At the last day?

**last day** Day of Judgement by God at the end of time

## The search for colonies

The continuing campaign against Catholic Spain during Elizabeth's reign is a reminder of the way in which economic as well as political issues were inextricably combined with religious disputes. Spain had led the way in the colonisation of the Americas. When Donne joined Essex's expedition to the Azores, the object had been to intercept a Spanish treasure fleet coming back from the Americas, which it failed to do. The exotic attractions of such conquests provide Donne with imagery to suggest the attractiveness of his mistress, as when he tells the sun in 'The Sun Rising' (lines 16–18):

Look, and tomorrow late, tell me,
Whether both the Indias of spice and mine
Be where thou left'st them, or lie here with me.

**Indias**   both the East and West Indies

The imagery is sometimes not only of riches, but also of conquest and possession, as here in 'To his Mistress Going to Bed' (lines 25–30):

License my roving hands, and let them go
Before, behind, between, above, below.
O my America, my new found land,
My kingdom, safeliest when with one man manned,
My mine of precious stones, my empery,
How blessed am I in this discovering thee!

**empery**   my empire

Having come late to colonisation, the English were eager to find territories that had not already been seized by the Spanish and Portuguese, but the first settlements in places such as Newfoundland and Virginia were unsuccessful, as was the search for an alternative trade route to the East via the 'Northwest Passage', north of America. There were, however, important advances in geographical knowledge. In 'Hymn to God my God, in my Sickness' (lines 6–15), Donne's comparison of himself on his sick bed to a map reflects a very topical interest:

Whilst my physicians by their love are grown
Cosmographers, and I their map, who lie
Flat on this bed, that by them may be shown
That this is my south-west discovery
*Per fretum febris,* by these straits to die,

I joy, that in these straits, I see my west;
For, though their currents yield return to none,
What shall my west hurt me? As west and east
In all flat maps (and I am one) are one,
So death doth touch the resurrectiön.

**Cosmographers**   map-makers
**my south-west**   south = heat of fever; west = decline of death
***Per fretum febris***   through the straits of fever (Latin)
**east**   east = resurrection

## Pressures for change in the reign of James I

The fact that Elizabeth I had never married had led to considerable concerns about the succession, but when she died in 1603 there was a peaceful transition of power as James VI of Scotland became James I of England. Although there was general relief at this, disappointment at the government's failure to relax laws against Catholics led in 1605 to the Gunpowder Plot, an unsuccessful attempt to blow up the Houses of Parliament.

Religious and political pressures did not only come from Roman Catholics. Like the Catholics, the Puritans were sure they knew what God's will was, and so were unable to make the kind of compromises required for the existence of a national Church embracing people of differing opinions about the nature of God and the way to worship him. Consequently there was increasing conflict within the Church of England. The only positive thing that emerged from a conference held at Hampton Court to try to resolve these disagreements was the decision that there should be a revised translation of the Bible. This was published in 1611 and is referred to either as the *Authorised Version* or the *King James Bible*.

The growth of belief in the Copernican theory that the earth revolved around the sun – and not the sun around the earth – was slow, but the publication in Latin of Galileo's *Sidereus Nuncius* (Star Messenger) in 1610, with its description of Galileo's observations through a telescope, ensured that the issue continued to be discussed. Donne famously observed that the 'new philosophy [science] calls all in doubt', but seemed happy to remain in doubt, whilst making use of the ideas. What he does appear to regret is that the observations of astronomers from the time of Ptolemy had disproved the concept of the perfectly spherical universe, with its symbolism of the harmony and order of God's creation, as this extract from 'An Anatomy of the World' (lines 251–257) illustrates:

> We think the heavens enjoy their spherical,
> Their round proportiön embracing all.
> But yet their various and perplexèd course,
> Observed in divers ages, doth enforce
> Men to find out so many eccentric parts,
> Such divers down-right lines, such overthwarts,
> As disproportion that pure form.

**various and perplexèd course**  i.e. the movement of the planets is not circular
**divers**  various
**eccentric**  off-centre
**down-right lines, such overthwarts**  lines running downwards and transversely

# Patronage and publication

For Donne, the only way to the kind of employment he was seeking was through the Court and the patronage of those with Court contacts. This explains a number of poems that seem very unattractive to modern readers because of their obsequious and flattering manner towards their recipients. Amongst the patrons from whom he sought support were Lucy, Countess of Bedford, and Magdalen Herbert, the mother of the poets George Herbert and Lord Herbert of Cherbury. In this example, praise of the Countess of Bedford is based on no less flattering a comparison than with God:

> Madam,
> Reason is our soul's left hand, Faith her right,
>   By these we reach divinity, that's you;
> Their loves, who have the blessing of your sight,
>   Grew from their reason, mine from fair faith grew.

Although individual poems were sometimes published to mark special occasions, before the Civil Wars it was not usual for poets to publish their poetry. This was partly a class issue, since many poets were not professional writers and it was felt rather vulgar to publish poetry that had originally been written to individuals or for friends to enjoy. Donne clearly felt that he had let himself down by publishing his 'Anniversaries': 'I confess I wonder how I declined [lowered myself] to it and do not pardon myself.' The fact that these poems were not intended for publication helps to explain why modern readers may find them so difficult and so **allusive**. However, a knowledge of the circumstances in which they were written often helps the reader's understanding and enjoyment. George Herbert had prepared his poems for possible publication, but when dying sent them to his friend Nicholas Ferrar with the message that they should only be published if he thought they might 'turn to the advantage of any dejected poor Soul'. It was only during the Commonwealth period that it became more normal to publish poetry, although even in the 1660s Katherine Philips was clearly worried that if, as a woman, she were to publish anything, she might appear to be pushing herself forward in an unseemly way.

## The Civil Wars

*Interesting that this is 'pendrip' but remembe Donne dies in 1631*

In 1633 William Laud was appointed Archbishop of Canterbury. His emphasis on ceremony in worship and on the importance of the sacrament of Holy Communion was seen by Puritans as a move back towards Roman Catholicism. Equally his insistence on strict Church discipline was seen as persecution. In 1620 the Pilgrim Fathers had sailed to North America to find religious freedom and in the 1630s more and more Puritans followed them. The cross currents of tension at the time can be seen in the fact that Herbert, a committed supporter of the Church of England's order, could imply sympathy with the Pilgrim Fathers when he wrote in 'The Church Militant': 'Religion stands on tip-toe in our land, / Ready to pass to the American strand'. The lines were almost censored when the poem was published in 1633.

When Charles I (reigned 1625–1649) attempted to impose the Church of England's *Book of Common Prayer* and new Church laws on the Scots, matters came to a head. The Scots rebelled, and Charles, who had been ruling without Parliament, was forced to summon a new Parliament in 1640 to raise money to put down the rebellion. This Parliament refused to co-operate and was soon dissolved, but a Scottish invasion forced Charles to call a second Parliament. Charles was unable to control either this second Parliament or the people of London. In 1642 he withdrew to Oxford and the Civil Wars began. Parliament succeeded in training an effective army and in establishing an alliance with the Scots. Charles was defeated and surrendered to the Scots in 1646. By this time, Archbishop Laud had been executed, and the celebration of Christmas and the use of the *Book of Common Prayer* had been forbidden.

In 1649, following a brief second Civil War, Charles I was tried and executed, the monarchy and House of Lords were abolished and the Commonwealth was proclaimed. Then, with Ireland in a state of rebellion and Scotland planning to crown Charles II, Parliament ordered the army to march against the Scots. It was at this point that the general of the Parliamentary army, Lord Fairfax, who had refused to take part in the trial of Charles I and who objected to attacking the Scots with whom a treaty had earlier been made, resigned. He retired to his estate at Nunappleton House, where he employed Andrew Marvell, who had been travelling on the Continent between 1642 and 1646, as tutor to his daughter, Mary. It was left to Cromwell first to reconquer Ireland in 1650 and then to defeat the Scots at the battle of Worcester. It was between these two campaigns that Marvell wrote 'An Horatian Ode upon Cromwell's Return from Ireland'. In this he shows respect for Charles's dignity at his execution ('He nothing common did or mean / Upon that memorable scene' – lines 57–58), but also a recognition of why Cromwell had defeated Charles (lines 37–40):

> Though justice against fate complain,
> And plead the ancient rights in vain:
>   But those do hold or break
>   As men are strong or weak.

Marvell also acknowledges Cromwell's virtue as well as his strength, since even the defeated Irish admit (lines 79–80):

> How good he is, how just,
> And fit for highest trust.

## The Commonwealth

The disturbances of the Civil Wars obviously affected the private lives of many who were less privileged than Fairfax. Over half the clergy, including Henry Vaughan's twin brother, Thomas, and the poet Robert Herrick, were ejected from their livings. They were driven out of their parishes and deprived of the income and house that went with the responsibility of looking after the parish. The loss of the regular pattern of worship was keenly felt by devout Anglicans, who had no reason to suppose that the Church of England would ever be re-established. Vaughan's indignation at the suppression of Christmas as a central Church festival and opportunity to give thanks for Christ's life on earth comes through strongly in the second part of 'Christ's Nativity' (lines 47–48) as does John Evelyn's in his diary entry for Christmas Day 1657 (see Part 3, page 99):

> Alas, my God! Thy birth now here
> Must not be numbered in the year.

It was in this climate of religious deprivation that, in different ways, both Henry Vaughan and Richard Crashaw drew inspiration from George Herbert's collected poems, *The Temple,* as Vaughan acknowledges in his preface to *Silex Scintillans* and Crashaw makes apparent in the title of his collection, *Steps to the Temple.*

While Vaughan, after his brief period of Royalist military service, returned home, for other poets the disruption brought by the Civil Wars was of a more drastic kind. Richard Crashaw fled to the Continent and converted to Roman Catholicism, while his friend Abraham Cowley (1618–1667), a fellow of Trinity College, Cambridge, abandoned academic life and spent ten years abroad doing intelligence work and other missions in the Royalist cause. A year after his return to England in 1654, he was arrested and imprisoned.

Some hint of the tensions caused by political and religious disagreements in private relationships can be sensed in the poetry of the Royalist-sympathising Katherine Philips, who was married to a successful Commonwealth politician. In this extract from 'To my Excellent Lucasia, on our Friendship' (lines 17–20), she compares the happiness of a husband or successful parliamentary general unfavourably with the delights of friendship:

*Later than Donne*

No bridegroom's nor crown-conqueror's mirth
  To mine compared can be:
They have but pieces of this earth,
  I've all the world in thee.

In contrast to the misfortunes and disappointments of Royalist poets, Marvell's career gradually took shape as the Commonwealth continued. From 1653, while tutoring William Dutton, he was staying at the house of John Oxenbridge, who had been deprived of his tutorship at Magdalen College, Oxford by Laud and had taken refuge in the Bermudas. Marvell's poem of this title illustrates the Puritan view of Laudian persecution, but in presenting the paradise-like quality of the island (lines 11–12, 25–32), he also reveals, intentionally or otherwise, the commercial value of the colony:

He lands us on a grassy stage,
Safe from the storms and prelate's rage.
...
With cedars, chosen by his hand,
From Lebanon, he stores the land,
And makes the hollow seas, that roar,
Proclaim the ambergris on shore.
He cast (of which we rather boast)
The gospel's pearl upon our coast,
And in these rocks for us did frame
A temple, where to sound his name.

**prelate**   priest of high rank, such as Laud
**ambergris**   valuable substance used in making perfumes
**gospel's pearl**   the precious Christian message
**frame**   make

Marvell's 'An Horatian Ode upon Cromwell's Return from Ireland' is so balanced that it has been claimed both as a poem hinting at Royalist sympathies and as being written by a newly convinced supporter of Cromwell. However, by the time that Marvell wrote 'The First Anniversary of the Government under his Highness the Lord Protector, 1655', his commitment to Cromwell and his respect for Cromwell's authority and energy are clear (lines 101–104):

And in his several aspects, like a star,
Here shines in peace, and thither shoots in war,
While by his beams observing princes steer,
And wisely court the influence they fear.

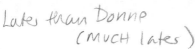
*Later than Donne*
*(MUCH later)*

**several aspects**  different positions in the sky with differing astrological 'influences'
**court**  pay attention to, like a courtier seeking favour
**influence**  also an astrological term for the effect of heavenly bodies on earthly matters

# The Restoration

In view of the uncertainty and confusion that followed the death of Cromwell,
Marvell may well have accepted the restoration of Charles II as the best political
solution available. However, it is not surprising to find that he is critical of the new
régime when he becomes convinced that the country is not being well governed.
After the successful Dutch raid on Chatham harbour in 1667, he wrote 'The Last
Instructions to a Painter', a satire in which metaphysical subtlety is replaced by a
direct and intentionally shocking assault on the immorality of Charles II's court.
This raid provided the context for the main purpose of the poem, a scathing
criticism of the political mismanagement and greed that led to this national
humiliation. This extract is from lines 978–980:

> ... scratching courtiers undermine a realm,
> And through the palace's foundations bore,
> Burrowing themselves to hoard their guilty store.

Two years later he wrote 'The Loyal Scot', which commemorated the heroic death
of Douglas in the Dutch attack on Chatham. In the poem, he also argued the
desirability of a parliamentary union between Scotland and England, and attacked
the Anglican clergy. Thus Marvell's later poems deal with political issues and
challenge corruption in government. Indeed, both these poems were published
anonymously out of fear for personal safety.

One poet who does not appear to have been especially troubled by the
Commonwealth was Thomas Traherne (1637–1764). In 1657 he was appointed
rector of Credenhill near Hereford by the Commonwealth Commissioners for the
Approbation of Public Preachers. When the bishops were reinstated at the
Restoration of Charles II, Traherne promptly had himself ordained deacon and
priest by a bishop. His unorthodox, visionary poetry expresses a confidence in the
goodness of the Creator and Creation, and appears untouched by the political
turmoil of the Civil Wars. In this extract from 'Shadows in the Water' (lines 77–80),
for example, he takes his mistaken childhood fancies about the 'other world' that he
sees reflected in a puddle as evidence of an ideal spiritual world that he will one day
reach:

> Some unknown joys there be
> Laid up in store for me;
> To which I shall, when that thin skin
> Is broken, be admitted in.

None of Traherne's poems was published during his lifetime and they would probably not have met with the approval of either the Puritans or the Church of England. Certainly his brother, Philip, who edited some of his poems after his death, but never published them, changed them quite ruthlessly to make them conform with religious 'correctness'.

Abraham Cowley's ode, 'To the Royal Society', published in 1667, shows how a quite different philosophic approach was becoming prevalent at this time. The Royal Society, a group of scientists and thinkers who had been meeting informally since the 1640s, was founded officially in 1660 at the Restoration. In his ode to the Society, Cowley praises the scientific method proposed by Francis Bacon earlier in the century in *The Advancement of Learning*. Bacon had said, 'Here is the first distemper [disease] of learning when men study words and not matter.' Cowley takes up the idea in lines 69–78 from the ode:

> From words, which are but pictures of the thought
> (Though we our thoughts from them perversely drew),
> To things, the mind's right object, he it brought;
> Like foolish birds to painted grapes we flew;
> He sought and gathered for our use the true;
> And when on heaps the chosen bunches lay,
> He pressed them wisely the mechanic way,
> Till all their juice did in one  vessel join,
> Ferment into a nourishment divine,
>     The thirsty soul's refreshing wine.

This 'wine' of scientific knowledge 'pressed … the mechanic way' is very different from the wine that Herbert had spoken of in 'The Agony' (lines 17–18), where Christ is the bunch of grapes and sin the press that forces out the juice of Christ's blood, which is also the Communion wine:

> Love is that liquor sweet and most divine,
> Which my God feels as blood; but I, as wine.

The new insistence on 'things' that science can analyse, rather than on abstract ideas expressed by 'words', helps to explain a loss of intensity in religious feeling after the Restoration – and also the relaxed way in which Cowley can view his friend

Crashaw's conversion to Catholicism. The downgrading of the importance of language (mere 'painted grapes') also helps to explain why Cowley's metaphysical use of language is entertaining, but often lacks the emotional urgency of the earlier metaphysical poets such as Herbert.

## Neo-platonism (Renaissance revival of classical thought)

One influential aspect of classical culture was the development of neo-platonism, that is ways of thinking derived from the ideas of the Greek philosopher, Plato (c428–346 BCE). Plato had taught that the endlessly changing physical universe of time and space was not real, but only a copy of a spiritual, ideal universe which was the true, unchanging and perfect reality. This was a belief that could be assimilated to the Christian concept of an ideal heaven and an imperfect earth, as Vaughan does in this extract from 'The World I' (lines 1–7):

> I saw Eternity the other night
> Like a great Ring of pure and endless light,
> All calm, as it was bright,
> And round beneath it, Time in hours, days, years
> Driven by the spheres
> Like a vast shadow moved, in which the world
> And all her train were hurled.

**train** all her followers

Plato describes those who fail to see beyond the material world to the ideal one as being like people in a cave with their backs to the entrance, who see only the shadows cast by a fire. They have no desire to be told that outside is the real world and the sun (symbolising absolute goodness). This image of the cave is also adapted by Vaughan (lines 49–54):

> O fools (said I) thus to prefer dark night
> Before true light,
> To live in grots, and caves, and hate the day
> Because it shows the way,
> The way which from this dead and dark abode
> Leads up to God.

The division between an ideal heaven and an earth which is an unreal and imperfect copy was related to Plato's teaching that the soul (the ideal, real part of a human being) comes from heaven and yearns to return there, since on earth it is trapped in the body and can see no more than mere 'shadows of eternity' (Vaughan

'The Retreat'). Similarly, Marvell's 'A Dialogue between the Soul and Body' shows the antipathy between a soul that longs for the spiritual reality of heaven and a body that is tied to this world. In 'The Garden' (lines 41–48) the concept is changed as Marvell describes how the soul may retreat into an internal world of its own:

> Meanwhile the mind, from pleasures less,
> Withdraws into its happiness:
> The mind, that ocean where each kind
> Does straight its own resemblance find;
> Yet it creates, transcending these,
> Far other worlds, and other seas,
> Annihilating all that's made
> To a green thought in a green shade.

Neo-platonist influences can also be seen in the writing of Thomas Traherne. In 'The Preparative' he describes the soul of the child in the womb as a 'living endless eye', a 'naked simple pure intelligence' capable of perceiving the **platonic** ideal (lines 24–25):

> Without disturbance then I did receive
> The fair ideas of all things.

Plato also suggested that men could be brought to love the ideal by ascending a 'ladder' or 'stair' that moves from love of an individual to love of physical beauty, moral beauty and finally to love of beauty itself. This spiritualising effect of love is adapted by Donne when he writes in lines 21–23 of 'The Ecstasy':

> If any, so by love refined,
> That he soul's language understood,
> And by good love were grown all mind …

The concept was combined with that of **courtly love,** in which the knightly lover idealises the woman and serves her, to produce the theory of 'platonic love', a sexless but spiritually intense union of minds.

A typically humorous and disrespectful use of neo-platonism occurs in 'The Good Morrow' (lines 6–7), when Donne brushes aside the fact that he has had other mistresses before his present mistress by suggesting tongue in cheek that they were unreal, mere copies of the platonic ideal represented by her beauty:

> If ever any beauty I did see,
> Which I desired and got, 'twas but a dream of thee.

Neo-platonism provided a series of ideas which writers could use, confident that their readers would recognise their allusions. It also presented a view of the universe in which all the parts were related and ordered, symbolised by the harmony of the music of the spheres which revolved around the earth carrying the sun, moon, planets and stars, an idea that Plato took up from Pythagoras (a Greek philosopher and mathematician of the 6th century BCE). Consequently it was a view which encouraged the development of **analogies** which is a key element of metaphysical style. So Donne's lovers in 'The Sun Rising' can be a microcosm, that is, a miniature copy of the world outside, and Vaughan's lovers in 'Amoret, of the Difference' are united by the same force that draws the compass to the north and keeps the planets in their places (lines 29–35):

> Thus to the north the loadstones move,
> And thus to them the enamoured steel aspires:
> > Thus, Amoret,
> > I do affect;
> And thus by wingèd beams, and mutual fire,
> > Spirits and stars conspire,
> > And this is LOVE.

**loadstones**  magnets
**affect**  love and aim towards like a compass

## Alchemy   *Early Science or crazy greed for gold & immortality*

The two great purposes of alchemy were to discover how to change base (non-precious) metals into gold by removing their impurities and similarly to discover a way of removing impurities from the human body to ensure long life, or even immortality. The agents for these changes were the philosopher's stone and the elixir of life. Whilst never achieving these aims, some alchemists did make significant discoveries and contributed to the development of pharmacy. Although many alchemists were sincere and in some cases advanced in learning, understandably human greed for wealth and immortality made alchemy a very effective weapon for fraudsters and con-men, and that in turn often made it a target for criticism. (The Canon's Yeoman tells of his master's tricks as an alchemist in Chaucer's tale of that name written in the 1390s, and there is also an amusing attack on such fraud in Ben Jonson's play *The Alchemist*.) Certainly when Donne refers to alchemy it is in a disparaging way, as in 'Love's Alchemy' where he is being cynical about love. Any pleasures that do derive from love, he argues (lines 6–12), are like the accidental by-products of an alchemical experiment; they are not true gold:

Oh, 'tis imposture all:
And as no chemic yet the elixir got,
But glorifies his pregnant pot,
If by the way to him befall
Some odoriferous thing, or medicinal,
So, lovers dream a rich and long delight,
But get a winter-seeming summer's night.

**imposture**  deception
**chemic**  alchemist
**pregnant**  productive
**If by the way ... medicinal**  if he creates by chance a sweet-smelling or
medicinal substance
**winter-seeming summer's night**  chilly, but also short

When Donne is praising love in 'The Sun Rising', he still uses alchemy to mean
something that only appears to be valuable, arguing that by comparison with the
richness of his love 'all wealth' is *mere* 'alchemy'. Similarly, when Herbert refers to
alchemy in 'The Elixir' (lines 21–24) it is specifically to reject it, saying that the true
elixir is to do everything for God's sake:

This is the famous stone
That turneth all to gold:
For that which God doth touch and own
Cannot for less be told.

**Cannot for less be told**  cannot be valued for less

Also important to alchemists was the attempt to extract the essence of substances,
'essence' being that which gives something its essential nature or being.
Something that had been refined or distilled five times in a retort or alembic (or
'limbeck' as Donne calls it) was a 'quintessence'. A good example of Donne's use of
these ideas can be found in 'A Nocturnal upon S. Lucy's Day'. Because the woman
whom he loves is dead he claims that love has 'wrought [performed] new alchemy'
and made him 'A quintessence even from nothingness'; 'I, by love's limbeck, am
the grave / Of all, that's nothing'; in other words his sorrow has distilled him down
to even less than nothing. Whereas the alchemists' aim was to establish the first
principle of life, love has brought him to the 'first nothing', the very essence of
death (lines 28–29):

But I am by her death (which word wrongs her)
Of the first nothing the elixir grown.

# Classical influences on metaphysical poetry

An important aspect of the Renaissance was the way in which writers exploited the fact that their readers had been educated to read Latin and were familiar with classical verse forms and themes. Classical forms therefore not only provided inspiration, but also a familiar norm against which variations could be made.

## Lyric

A common theme of lyric love poetry is *carpe diem,* often translated as 'seize the day' and meaning 'pick the day like a ripe fruit', in other words enjoy yourself while you can before the fruit of pleasure rots. It is an argument frequently used by male writers urging a woman to give in to their sexual advances. Here it is used by the Roman poet Catullus (c 84–54 BCE) in a poem addressed to Lesbia *(Carmina* V) and adapted by Ben Jonson:

> Come my Celia, let us prove,
> While we may, the sports of love;
> Time will not be ours, for ever:
> He, at length, our good will sever.
> Spend not then his gifts in vain.
> Suns that set may rise again,
> But if once we lose this light,
> 'Tis, with us, perpetual night.

**prove**  test by experience

What Jonson has taken from Catullus in the last three lines is not simply the idea of death being an unending night, but also the terseness which gives the idea such an uncomfortable impact. Jonson's translation is a close and effective one, but the interest in studying sources is not merely in seeing how certain classical themes are repeated, but in seeing how they are modified, since this process of comparison helps to identify what makes a poem unique rather than just an imitation.

▶ Compare Jonson's adaptation with lines 21–32 from 'To His Coy Mistress' by Andrew Marvell (Part 3, page 83). What has Marvell added to the original? You may feel that the lines starting 'But at my back' capture a similar sense of urgency to that in Jonson's translation of Catullus, but what happens after that? However you react to the next lines (reactions include finding them amusing or offensive), there can be little doubt that the traditional *carpe diem* argument is being treated in a different way. (There is further discussion of this poem on page 110.)

# Elegy

The most common modern meaning of elegy, and the original one, is a lament for the dead, but the elegies, *Amores,* of the Roman poet Ovid (43 BCE–17 CE) are so called simply because their verse form (elegiac couplets) is the same as that used in Greek and Latin for poems of mourning, despite the fact that their subject matter is love. Ovid's poems trace a stormy, extra-marital affair with a girl called Corinna with sexual frankness and cynicism, and it is Ovid that Donne chooses to imitate in his elegies in a conscious reaction against the idealised love poetry of his time.

When Ovid's *Amores* were translated by Christopher Marlowe (1564–1593) as *Ovid's Elegies* they were the least well known of his works to the Elizabethans. The fact that his translation was printed at least six times in the 1590s and that one edition was burnt on the orders of the Bishop of London, is evidence of the excitement that it caused at the time. Donne must have been interested not only in the daring subject matter, but also the polished use of rhyming couplets and of a much more direct tone than was normal in poetry at the time. Typical of the tone are lines 17–20 and 35–36 from Elegy 4 in Book 1 in which 'Ovid' (i.e. the 'I' of the poem) gives his mistress advice about how to receive his advances when attending a banquet with her husband, whilst also expressing a suspicious fear that she may be willing to accept her own husband's amorous advances:

> View me, my becks and speaking countenance,
> Take and receive each secret amorous glance.
> Words without voice shall on my eyebrows sit,
> Lines thou shalt read in wine by my hand writ.
> ...
> Let not thy neck by his vile arms be pressed,
> Nor lean thy soft head on his boist'rous breast.

> **becks and speaking countenance**  gestures and expressive face

Donne echoes this in his Elegy 7 (lines 1–6) in which he regrets having taught a woman the codes of love which she now uses to communicate with others:

> Nature's lay idiot, I taught thee to love,
> And in that sophistry, oh, thou dost prove
> Too subtle: Fool, thou didst not understand
> The mystic language of the eye nor hand:
> Nor couldst thou judge the difference of the air
> Of sighs, and say, this lies, this sounds despair.

> **Nature's lay idiot**  stupidly ignorant of how you would naturally behave
> **sophistry**  crafty skill

More important than any specific poem, however, is Ovid's general example of writing about love without inhibitions and with an immediacy that echoes the speaking voice. In 'The Sun Rising', for example, it is not just that Donne echoes Ovid (*Amores* I, 13) in telling the sun to go away and let his night of love continue, but the fact that the lovers being in bed together is taken for granted. Ovid's influence is also apparent in cynical poems such as Donne's 'The Indifferent' ('I can love both fair and brown').

## Epigram

The epigram is a poem that makes its point in very few words. It is the slightest of all classical forms to influence Renaissance writers, but its very brevity challenges the writer to use **wit** in an almost metaphysical way in order to pack meaning in, as in this translation by Richard Lovelace (1618–1658) of Catullus's Carmina LXXXV about the paradoxical feelings of the lover:

> I hate and love, wouldst thou the reason know?
> I know not, but I burn and feel it so.

The epigram form was also adapted by the Jesuits as a means of conveying religious ideas in a punchy and memorable manner. Richard Crashaw in turn copied the Jesuits in a series of brief poems reflecting on passages from the Bible, such as this one on how Mary Magdalene washes Christ's feet with her tears and dries them with her red hair:

> Her eyes' flood licks his feet's fair stain,
> Her hair's flame licks up that again.
> This flame thus quenched hath brighter beams:
> This flood thus stainèd, fairer streams.

> **hair's flame** her red hair

Here again the poem relies on **paradox:** because the 'stain' is dust from the feet of Christ it actually makes Mary's hair 'brighter' and her tears of regret for sin 'fairer'.

## Other influential classical verse forms

Both Donne and Marvell wrote satire, but classical satire provides a precedent for various qualities that are typical of a much wider range of metaphysical poetry, such as the use of colloquial language, wit and **irony,** the intention to shock and a strong sense of the poet's individual personality. The epistle (verse letter) with its slightly informal letter-writing style provides another model for the expression of personal ideas and experiences, as in Donne's letters to Sir Henry Wotton.

Odes are short lyrical pieces in a variety of verse forms which deal with a variety of subjects including politics. The odes of the Roman poet, Horace (65–8 BCE), provide a model, or at any rate a point of comparison, for Marvell's 'An Horatian Ode upon Cromwell's Return from Ireland'. Horace fought on the losing side as a republican against Augustus, the first Roman emperor, in the civil war that followed the assassination of Julius Caesar in 44 BCE, but then received patronage and protection from Augustus. Marvell reverses this situation as a poet who can feel sympathy for the defeated Charles I, but who recognises the need for Cromwell's 'indefatigable' rule to prevail (see page 26).

At first sight pastoral poetry, set in a peaceful, idealised countryside in which characters engage in singing competitions, seems escapist. However, Virgil's *Eclogues* were also written just after the civil war that followed the assassination of Julius Caesar. Caesar's heirs had won the war and then rewarded their soldiers by giving them farms in the region where Virgil lived. Virgil was lucky in his contacts and had his land given back to him, but in his opening poem one of the characters has been forced off his land. Like Horace's odes, therefore, pastoral poems may seem escapist advertisements for the attractions of the good life in the countryside, but to anyone troubled by the gap between the ideal and the actual state of affairs (not only Royalists who had lost their lands after the Civil Wars) they were capable of carrying more serious meanings.

## Assignments

1   Choose two or three poems by metaphysical poets that throw light on the politics of the time and show how they do this.

2   Compare the attitude to sin and forgiveness in Wotton's 'A Hymn to my God in a Night of my Late Sickness' (Part 3, page 96) and in Donne's 'A Hymn to God the Father' (Part 3, page 72), and some of his Divine Meditations such as 'Oh my black soul' and 'Batter my heart'. What evidence is there of Wotton's Protestant faith? Is the evidence as convincing in Donne's case?

3   Read the extract from Ovid's *Elegies* (page 83) and compare it with some of Donne's love poems. In what ways are Donne's poems similar in attitude to that shown in the Ovid extract and what else do they express?

# Approaching the poems

- What should you look out for when reading a metaphysical poem?

- What do you learn about relationships between the sexes from the love poetry?

- How do the religious ideas of the period influence the poetry?

- How do the metaphysical poets react to public and political events?

Metaphysical poetry explores many topics, ranging from human relationships in love, friendship and death, and relationships with the Christian God, to politics and social issues, but above all it reflects the truth about human experience. This is just as true of the religious poetry, which deals with such emotions as love, elation, fear, guilt and remorse, as it is of the love poetry, the elegies, the verse letters and the satires.

## Language, tone and poetic technique

There are some direct questions that need to be answered when reading any poem:

- What at first sight is this poem about?

- What techniques has the poet used to express thought and feeling?

In your first reading of a poem you will need to establish a basic understanding of the poem's meaning. Do you understand the vocabulary used? You will not only need to check on unfamiliar words, but also that the meanings of familiar ones have not changed. Are there any puns to convey double meanings or to hint at contradictions? Does the **syntax** create ambiguity or put emphasis on a particular word? Does the order or sound of the words make them more dramatic to speak?

Intertwined with these basic questions will be questions about the tone of the poetry. Is it colloquial or formal, personal or public? In what ways does the sound of the poetry – for example, rhythm, rhyme, alliteration and pattern – affect the tone or reinforce the meaning? (It is important to read the poetry out loud.) Is the imagery learned or homely, worked out simply or developed in elaborate detail? Are there paradoxes and if so do they reflect personal doubts or are they an integral part of the material which the poet is working on (especially the paradoxes of Christianity). Are there different 'layers' of meaning? Do different meanings reinforce each other or generate irony?

A number of these points can be illustrated by a reading of one of Donne's most carefully structured poems, his 'Divine Sonnet 14'. Here are the first four lines:

> Batter my heart, three-personed God; for, you
> As yet but knock, breathe, shine, and seek to mend;
> That I may rise, and stand, o'erthrow me, and bend
> Your force, to break, blow, burn, and make me new.

The vigour of the language is immediately apparent with its many monosyllabic verbs of action contrasting with the abstract theological definition of the God who is being asked to perform these actions as 'three-personed' (in other words, God as Father, Son and Holy Spirit). It is not only the verbs that suggest vigour, but also the rhythm. The underlying rhythm appears to be iambic (i.e. each weak syllable is followed by a stressed one, as in 'my héart, three-pérsoned Gód'). However, this is challenged from the start with the opening word 'Batter', appropriately starting with a strongly stressed syllable followed by a weaker one. Even the most regularly iambic line here, line 3, has an extra syllable thrown in ('me'), which adds to the sense of breathless urgency of the poem. Despite the opening's lack of rhythmic regularity, it is nevertheless very carefully structured. Each verb in line 2 is matched by a similar but more forceful one in line 4, and here again the iambic rhythm breaks down as the monosyllabic verbs of lines 2 and 4 follow each other without any weak syllables in between, like hammer blows on an anvil. Line 4 with the stronger verbs is also given further energy by the use of alliterative 'b' sounds. A further effect is created by enjambment, that is by allowing the sense to run on from one line to another without pause, as happens at the end of both lines 1 and 3. And what is the object of all this energy? – the paradox that Donne, with an urgency bordering on desperation, sees that his only hope of *standing* amongst those saved by God is that God should first *overthrow* him and all his sins (line 3).

This idea is then developed in the image of a besieged city held by the 'enemy' (the Devil) because Donne's reason, which should be ruling as God's deputy (his 'viceroy'), lacks the strength to resist sin, despite the fact that Donne loves God. The 'battering' is now not simply that of the blacksmith, but of a battering ram:

> I, like an usurped town, to another due,
> Labour to admit you, but oh, to no end,
> Reason your viceroy in me, me should defend,
> But is captived, and proves weak or untrue,
> Yet dearly I love you, and would be lovèd fain,
> But am betrothed unto your enemy ...

**usurped**  properly belonging to another, in other words, God
**to no end**  to no avail
**would be lovèd fain**  would wish to be loved

Here, despite the detailed working out of the comparison between the besieged city and Donne, the tone of voice remains urgent in the regretful exclamation: 'but oh, to no end'. Consider also what the effect is when the syntax is structured in such a way as to repeat the word 'me'; does it reflect self-importance, or panic, or something else?

By the last two lines quoted above the image has changed again. At the time, the soul was regarded as feminine, and Donne's soul now requests a more shocking assault than that of the blacksmith's hammer or the battering ram:

> Divorce me, untie, or break that knot again,
> Take me to you, imprison me, for I
> Except you enthral me, never shall be free,
> Nor ever chaste, except you ravish me.

*betrothed—ised*
*maybe promised*
*even intended*
*but not yet consummated*
*married*

**that knot**   the knot of a marriage obligation to the Devil

The impact of the final paradox is so strong that it is easy to overlook the need to check the meaning of 'enthral' in the penultimate line. Two meanings combine here to enhance the sense: the original meaning of 'to enslave', which brings out the paradox that only when he is enslaved by God can he be free (to serve God is 'perfect freedom' according to *The Book of Common Prayer*), and the secondary meaning of 'to attract strongly'. The reversal of grammatical structure also adds to the impact, with the two clauses beginning 'except you' sandwiching 'never shall be free, / Nor ever chaste'. Not only does this draw attention to the key point that Donne is dependent on God's taking the initiative; it also achieves a dramatic effect by postponing the shocking image of ravishment until the very end of the poem (but note that 'ravish' can also mean to transport the soul to heaven in ecstasy while leaving the body behind).

Regardless of whether you accept all the suggestions made above, the ability to read a poem in such a way is a necessary preliminary to appreciating it. However, it is an incomplete approach because it either takes for granted, or fails to consider at all, such matters as what light the religious and biographical context can throw on the poem, or what view a woman – or indeed a man – might take of the image of rape for divine possession.   *Interesting distinction – also interesting ravish=rape*

In addition to looking at the workings of poetry in terms of vocabulary, grammatical structure, patterning and sound effects, it is important to become familiar with the device which is often thought of as being most typically 'metaphysical', the metaphysical conceit. The comparison of two things which are apparently quite different and the demonstration that they do after all have a significant similarity is not merely an exercise of ingenuity, although the combination of ingenuity and knowledge known as wit plays a large part in it. For example, Donne's comparison of himself on his sick bed to a map in 'Hymn to God my God, in my Sickness' (Part 1, page 23) is not just a simple comparison of the doctors bending over his body to navigators bending over a map. It goes beyond this to make a point about the Christian belief that death leads to new life in resurrection, just as the most westerly point on the map is actually right next to the most easterly point because the earth is round. Imagery of this kind is different from that in much poetry. It is often part of a reasoned argument rather than a description (we never learn, for example, what Donne's mistresses look like) and so its appeal is to the intellect rather than the imagination. Understanding such imagery can sometimes seem like decoding a crossword clue, and that can be part of the pleasure of the poetry, but there is always a danger that in the pursuit of an image's abstract meaning the reader will become blind to other implications of the image. Is it, for example, sufficient to read the last two lines of 'Batter my Heart' and just see them as a reference to the Christian belief that to serve God is 'perfect freedom', or does the shocking image of rape oblige us to consider whether by **deconstructing** the poem a different understanding will emerge?

*[handwritten margin note: Compare Shakespeare]*

*[handwritten note: Balance? both possible?]*

## Verse forms

Another important aspect of metaphysical poetry is the wide range of verse forms used. In the late 16th-century, the dominant form for love poetry became the fourteen-line **sonnet**, usually with lines of ten syllables, based on the poems of Petrarch (1304–1374) and introduced into English through the translations and imitations of poets such as the Earl of Surrey (1517?–1547). Part of the reaction against **Petrarchan** writing (see pages 44–46) was to abandon this form in favour of rhyming couplets, although Donne continued to use the sonnet for most of his religious poems (as in the example above), as did Herbert occasionally. Another feature of Donne's writing was to break away from the careful rhythmical patterns of much Elizabethan poetry and write in a deliberately rough manner that aimed to capture the emotional tone of the speaking voice. Examples are the openings of 'Batter my Heart' and of 'The Good Morrow', in which the apparent regularity of the first line is overridden by the dramatic rush of words: 'I wonder by my troth, what thou and I / Did, till we loved?'

At the same time the metaphysicals developed a much wider range of verse forms in which the length of both lines and verses could be varied. Some were derived from earlier verse forms such as those used by Philip and Mary Sidney in their psalm translations of the 1580s and 1590s, but many, especially in Herbert's case, were original. This variety of form enabled Herbert at times to match verse form and meaning very closely, as in the opening of 'Easter'. Here the shortness of the second line brings back the rhyme sound 'Without delays' and expresses Herbert's meaning exactly:

> Rise heart; thy Lord is risen. Sing his praise
> > Without delays.

On occasion the form matched the meaning in a different way when the pattern on the page was itself used to reinforce the meaning, as in 'Easter-wings'. Herbert's forms, although immensely varied, remain consistent from verse to verse within the poem, except where there is a deliberate change, such as the hymn at the end of 'Easter' (Part 3, page 78) or the introduction of the final rhyme to make the point at the end of 'Denial' (Part 3, page 77). Crashaw and Vaughan sometimes aim for still greater flexibility, using irregular forms to express the spontaneity of religious emotion, as in the opening of Vaughan's 'The Morning Watch':

> O joys! Infinite sweetness! With what flowers,
> And shoots of glory, my soul breaks, and buds!
> > All the long hours
> > Of night, and rest
> > Through the still shrouds
> > Of sleep, and clouds,
> This dew fell on my breast;
> > O how it bloods,
> And spirits all my earth! Hark! In what rings,
> And hymning circulations the quick world
> > Awakes, and sings;

Rhyming couplets were used as an equivalent to Latin elegiac couplets not only in love elegies, but also as a suitably dignified form for elegies for the dead – for example, see the extract from Henry King's elegy on his wife on page 52. They also provided a convenient form for some of Donne's verse letters and were used in a variety of ways in satire. Donne aims to create a rough naturalness of tone that at times quite ignores the couplet as a unit, as in the opening of Satire 2:

> Sir, though (I thank God for it) I do hate
> Perfectly all this town, yet there's one state
> In all ill things so excellently best, ...

By comparison Marvell is happy to match the neatly contained form of the couplet with each satirical jibe, as in this description from 'The Last Instructions to a Painter', (lines 29–32) of the Duke of St Albans, who was rumoured to be a lover of the Queen Mother:

Paint then St Albans full of soup and gold,
The new court's pattern, stallion of the old.
Him neither wit nor courage did exalt,
But Fortune chose him for her pleasure salt.

**pattern**  example
**salt**  lustful


# Love poetry

## Reactions to Petrarch

In the 1590s it would have been impossible to read or write love poetry without
being aware of the translations and imitations of the love sonnets of the Italian
poet, Petrarch. One key feature of these poems is the distress of the male poet
wounded by the arrow of Cupid, the blind, winged boy who was the god of love and
whose arrows of love were often fired from the beloved's bright eyes. The cruelty of
the beloved woman – usually, in fact, her insistence on chastity – leads to the
lover's suffering extremes of torment. Another common device is for the lover to
make a list (a blazon) of each of the beloved's beauties with appropriate
comparisons. *(NB 12th Night Olivia )*

Shakespeare's *Romeo and Juliet* (first produced in about 1595) provides a
commentary on Petrarchan love conventions such as these. At the start of the play,
the immature Romeo only thinks that he is in love and in typically Petrarchan
manner describes himself as being 'sore enpierced' with a 'shaft' shot from Cupid's
bow. However, when Romeo sees Juliet and falls truly in love, Shakespeare does not
abandon Petrarchan language, but instead uses it at a new level of intensity. For
example when Juliet appears on the balcony, Romeo calls Juliet the sun ('But soft!
What light through yonder window breaks? / It is the east, and Juliet is the sun!')
and goes on to suggest that her eyes are brighter than the stars.

*Compare Sun Rising*

Before this scene, however, comes Mercutio's mockery of Romeo's earlier
immature love. Mercutio is satirical about the hackneyed images of love poetry
('couple but "love" and "dove"') and parodies the Petrarchan listing of the beloved's
features, ending in Act II, scene 1 (lines 17–20) with a most un-Petrarchan hint
that all the fine talk about the lady's beauty boils down to lust:

I conjure thee by Rosaline's bright eyes,
By her high forehead, and her scarlet lip,
By her fine foot, straight leg, and quivering thigh,
And the demesnes that there adjacent lie ...

**conjure**  summon
**demesnes**  regions

*[handwritten top:]* Petrarch — much imitated by Early Elizabethans
but — not only hollow conventions

Like Shakespeare, Donne is very aware of the Petrarchan style, but deliberately uses some of its features to create an anti-Petrarchan effect. For example, he accepts the convention that the beloved's eyes are as bright as the sun or the stars in order to exploit it in a compressed and light-hearted way. Thus in 'The Sun Rising', he tells off the sun for disturbing him in bed with his mistress (not a Petrarchan situation!) and says in passing, 'If her eyes have not blinded thine', thus casually implying that his mistress's eyes are bright enough to dazzle the sun itself. The same type of **hyperbole** is seen in 'The Dream', when Donne suggests that it must have been the brightness of the woman's eyes that awoke him when she came to him at night.

In a different way, the overt sexuality of Elegy 19, 'To his Mistress Going to Bed', can be seen not simply as imitating Ovid's view of sex (see page 36), but also as a reaction against the Petrarchan convention of the devoted and submissive male and his chaste mistress (the 'whining poetry' that Donne scorns himself for writing in 'The Triple Fool'). Urging the woman to remove one item of clothing after another to reveal the beauties underneath, he expands the subversively lustful idea hinted at in the last line of Mercutio's parody of the Petrarchan custom of listing each of the woman's beauties. *[handwritten:]* Self mockery also — evident in many of his

Donne's poetry does not, however, only celebrate the delights of love. When it deals with its frustrations, it does so in a variety of ways. Sometimes he assumes a tone of off-hand cynicism, as in 'The Indifferent' ('I can love both fair and brown'), but in 'Twicknam Garden' (lines 1–6) he chooses to use a further typically Petrarchan convention of contrasting the calm of nature with the torment of the lover:

> Blasted with sighs, and surrounded with tears,
>   Hither I come to seek the spring,
>   And at mine eyes, and at mine ears,
> Receive such balms, as else cure everything;
>   But O, self traitor, I do bring
> The spider love; ...

Compare this with the opening of an adaptation of a Petrarch sonnet by Surrey in which again the unhappy lover is surrounded by the quiet beauty of nature:

> Alas, so all things now do hold their peace,
> Heaven and earth disturbèd in no thing;
> The beasts, the air, the birds their song do cease;
> The night's car the stars about doth bring.
> Calm is the sea, the waves work less and less.
> So am not I, whom love, alas, doth wring ...

**The night's car... bring**  the stars pull round night's chariot
**wring**  torture

*[handwritten right margin:]* conventional declarations. he is BEYOND convention or the males he applies conventional hyperbole REALITY! or he applies We convention but smiles, sometimes the fully, as he does

▶ What strikes you as distinctive about each of these approaches to disappointment in love?

Not all of Donne's love poetry, however, is cynical, erotic or tormented. 'Sweetest love, I do not go / For weariness of thee' (Part 3, page 69), which Donne's biographer, Isaac Walton, thought was written before he parted from his wife on a journey to the Continent in 1611, has a tone of tender concern. 'The Autumnal', with its praise of an older woman's appearance, including her wrinkles, is also very different in tone from Petrarchan poetry, which promises to preserve youthful beauty in immortal verse in defiance of physical decay.

Those of Donne's poems that attempt to persuade the beloved to give in to the desires of the lover are, of course, in one sense following Petrarchan tradition, but the difference is that the proposal is often made with a frank sexuality and also an expectation of success that would be deemed improper in a Petrarchan poem. In tone, they are much closer to Ovid's elegies, while often using the *carpe diem* argument of lyric poets like Catullus (see page 35). These poems frequently have a dramatic immediacy that not only echoes Ovid, but can also be found in the poems of Donne's playwright contemporary, Ben Jonson. This extract is from 'Begging Another, on Colour of Mending the Former' (lines 1–4):

> For love's sake, kiss me once again,
>   I long, and should not beg in vain,
>     Here's none to spy, or see;
>       Why do you doubt, or stay?

If this is compared, for example, with Donne's 'The Flea', it can be seen that it is the use of the conceit that makes Donne's poem distinctively metaphysical. Although the situation and the colloquial tone may be similar in both poems, there is nothing remotely comparable in Jonson's poem to the far-fetched suggestion that the flea 'our marriage bed, and marriage temple is' because it has already united their blood by biting both lovers.

## Platonic love

The ideal of a platonic, spiritualised love in which sex played no part (see page 32) appears in many of the Petrarchan sonnet sequences and it continued to be a feature of love poetry in the 17th century. Such a love is sometimes seen as entirely separate from sexual love and sometimes valued as a component of a love that combines the physical and spiritual. Donne sees it as the latter in 'A Valediction: Forbidding Mourning' (lines 21–24), in which it provides assurance that the lovers' physical separation cannot separate their spiritual love:

> Our two souls, therefore, which are one,
>   Though I must go, endure not yet
> A breach, but an expansïon,
>   Like gold to aery thinness beat.

**aery**  not only 'airy', but also spiritual rather than physical

Edward Herbert's 'Ode upon a Question Moved, Whether Love Should Continue for Ever?' also celebrates platonic love, but sees it as self-sufficient. The poem finishes (lines 149–152) with an affirmation that platonic love will outlast death and leaves the lovers in a state of spiritual union, but physical passivity:

> While such a moveless silent peace
>   Did seize on their becalmèd sense,
>   One would have thought some influence
> Their ravished spirits did possess.

**moveless**  motionless
**influence**  astrological influence of the stars

There is a similar moment in 'The Ecstasy' (lines 14–20; for full text see Part 3, page 66) when the souls of the two lovers are experiencing an ecstasy – in the original sense of being in a trance outside their bodies:

> Our souls (which to advance their state,
>   Were gone out) hung 'twixt her, and me.
>
> And whilst our souls negotiate there,
>   We like sepulchral statues lay;
> All day, the same our postures were,
>   And we said nothing, all the day.

Significantly, however, this physical passivity comes near the beginning. Spiritual love by itself is not enough for the speaker of Donne's poem: 'Love's mysteries in souls do grow, / But yet the body is his book'. In other words, the spiritual mystery of love needs to be expressed by being written, as it were, in the book of the body.

A generation later, Katherine Philips was to reassert the value of platonic love in her poems of female friendship. In her poem 'To Mrs Mary Aubrey at Parting' (lines 19–24), she writes that their 'changed and mingled souls' can no longer be separated from each other:

> And thus we can no absence know,
>   Nor shall we be confined;

Our active souls will daily go
　To learn each other's mind.
Nay, should we never meet to sense
Our souls would hold intelligence.

**never meet to sense**　never meet where we can see, hear and touch
**hold intelligence**　communicate with each other

However, the idealistic lack of concern at physical absence ('should we never meet to sense' – like Donne's lovers who 'Care less eyes, lips, and hands to miss' in 'A Valediction: Forbidding Mourning') is shown to be unsustainable in a subsequent poem ('To Mrs M.A. upon Absence', lines 13–16):

What angry star then governs me
　That I must feel a double smart?
Prisoner to fate as well as thee;
　Kept from thy face, linked to thy heart?

Marvell's approach to love poetry is hard to define. His treatment of the *carpe diem* theme in 'To His Coy Mistress' (Part 3, pages 83–84; see also page 110) has attracted much discussion, but some critics have commented on the lack of any sense of the beloved's presence. This is even more the case in 'The Definition of Love', which defines a perfect – and in some sense platonic – love as being by definition one that nobody could hope would ever exist: 'begotten by Despair / Upon Impossibility'. The same sense of detachment is apparent in 'Mourning'. The main part of the poem puts forward a number of cynical explanations for the woman's tears which are then rejected at the end, in lines 29–36:

How wide they dream! The Indian slaves
That dive for pearl through seas profound
Would find her tears yet deeper waves
And not of one the bottom sound.

I yet my silent judgement keep,
Disputing not what they believe:
But sure as oft as women weep,
It is to be supposed they grieve.

However, the ambiguity makes this apparent defence of women less than convincing. Is 'sound' a verb meaning 'to measure the depth by reaching the bottom' as seems likely on a first reading, or does it mean that not one of her tears is 'sound', meaning trustworthy, all the way through? Similarly 'It is to be supposed' is ambiguous. Is it 'Women should be given the benefit of the doubt', or – if 'supposed' is ironically stressed – 'You ought to believe that women grieve even if you really know better'?

If Marvell's own judgement is 'silent' here, the woman's is still more so. There is no opportunity for defence against a stereotype. However, it is not simply as a reaction to unfairness that some gender criticism focuses on the silence of the woman's voice in most male love poetry. It is also to open up new readings of poetry written by men.

## The woman's voice

*Sidney's Nece*

It is only quite recently that much women's poetry of this period has been found and published. Even now there is relatively little available. Consequently, the woman's role is mostly seen through the eyes of men. One woman, however, who did write poetry was Lady Mary Wroth (1586–1651?). Although she chose the old-fashioned medium of a sonnet sequence for her *Pamphilia to Amphilanthus,* following the examples of her father and uncle, Robert and Philip Sidney, she used the sequence to create a space for a female **persona** that may seem natural enough to us, but had no precedent at the time. The direct address to a critical friend at the opening of her Sonnet 45 ('Good now, be still, and do not me torment / With multitudes of questions' – see Part 3, page 98) can be seen as following models such as Donne's 'The Canonization' ('For God's sake hold your tongue, and let me love'). Yet the idea that her distress is because she is 'possessed ... [by] The hellish spirit, Absence' (the absence of the male lover about his masculine business) provides an expression of the elsewhere unspoken thoughts that women such as the recipient of Donne's 'A Valediction: Forbidding Mourning' might be presumed to have. Significantly, the one Donne poem written from the woman's angle, 'Break of Day', makes just the same point in lines 13 and 17–18:

Must business thee from hence remove?
...
He which hath business, and makes love, doth do
Such wrong, as when a married man doth woo.

Wroth's situation was unusual because she was born into a wealthy and aristocratic family and had exceptional educational opportunities: her father was later to be Earl of Leicester, and her aunt was Mary Sidney, translator of the Psalms. Nor did Wroth match the ideal image put forward in male writings of the obedient, silent and chaste woman. Not only did she publish her writings, but she also had two children by her cousin William Herbert, Earl of Pembroke, after the death of her husband. Most women of the time did not enjoy such freedom. For one thing, marriages were financial transactions in which the women had little say. A marriage portion or dowry would be settled on their husband when they married, but they had no rights to any property once they had married unless their husbands died before them (less common then because of the risks of childbirth). In a play of 1621, *Women Beware Women*, one of the women observes, 'Men buy their slaves, but women buy their masters' (Act 1, scene 2).

In a world where riches were for male possession, it seems reasonable to assume that the female reader might well have had a fairly cynical view of imagery which equates the woman with wealth ('both the Indias of spice and mine' in 'The Sun Rising') and of the claim that possession is mutual ('Let us possess one world, each hath one, and is one' in 'The Good Morrow'). In her poem 'To my Excellent Lucasia', it may be that Katherine Philips is not only rating her love for her friend Lucasia far above that which any husband can feel – 'They [husbands] have but pieces of this earth, / I've all the world in thee' – but is also implying that the man's interest in his wife is really an interest in the property that she brings as a dowry – 'pieces ... of this earth' (for full text, see Part 3, page 90).

The other major matter that must have influenced any real woman's response to all those poems urging a woman to give in to the poet's wish that she should sleep with him was the importance that men, as well as women, set on chastity. After all, if a woman was not a virgin at marriage and faithful to her husband thereafter, how could he be sure that his property would be inherited by a true heir? When Ben Jonson praises Wroth's father, Sir Robert Sidney, in his poem about his house and household, 'To Penshurst', he includes praise of his wife's ability to bear children (she is 'fruitful') and of her faithfulness, but in doing so he cannot refrain from the insulting suggestion that such faithfulness is uncommon (lines 90–92):

> Thy lady's noble, fruitful, chaste withal.
> His children thy great lord may call his own:
> A fortune, in this age, but rarely known.

**Thy** the house's – the poem is addressed to the house

The Biblical justification for this assumption that women were a dangerous temptation to men was that it was all Eve's fault that Adam ate the apple and ensured humanity's expulsion from Paradise. Another woman writer, Aemilia Lanyer (1569–1645), attacks this argument with some subtlety in *Salve Deus Rex Iudaeorum* (Part 3, page 82). She accepts the argument that men are intellectually superior (difficult for the men to disagree with!), but uses this to argue that Adam's sin was the greater since he knew what he was doing, whereas Eve's fault 'was only too much love'. Furthermore, men like to boast of their knowledge, 'which he took

/ From Eve's fair hand, as from a learned book'.

Katherine Philips's reaction to claims of masculine superiority was to argue that souls do not have sexes and that therefore the highest form of love, platonic love between souls, is not the exclusive domain of men, but can be found in friendships between women. This extract is from 'A Friend' (lines 19–22):

> If souls no sexes have, for men to exclude
>   Women from friendship's vast capacity,
> Is a design injurious and rude,
>   Only maintained by partial tyranny.

On a more down-to-earth level she offers brisk mockery of unwanted male advances in 'To Sir Amorous La Foole' (lines 13–18):

> What pretty dotage call you this,
> To weep and groan and glance and kiss;
> Unkindness makes your heart to break,
> And not a word of sense to speak,
> And court the Careless, when with far less pain,
> Some wholesome milkmaid would say yours again.

> **dotage**  in other words, the besotted behaviour of the love-sick male
> **Careless**  the woman who doesn't care for you
> **say yours again**  say she was yours

▶ Given male attitudes to women and that women faced social ruin if they were unchaste, and bearing in mind the attitudes revealed by Lanyer and Philips, how is your reading of poems such as Donne's 'The Flea' and Marvell's 'To His Coy Mistress' affected?

## Love beyond death: the elegy

The publication of elegies, poems on the death of a friend, relation or public figure, may seem rather artificial, because as formal public responses they lack the spontaneity that a modern reader might associate with grief. However, it is worth remembering that control and organisation of feeling are necessary requirements of all art, even when the intention is to create an appearance of spontaneity.

Carew's elegy on Donne (Part 3, page 65) is a fine example of a tribute to the gifts of the dead person being commemorated, as is Cowley's elegy for Richard Crashaw. Cowley acknowledges the difference in belief (Crashaw became Roman Catholic towards the end of his life) with affectionate tolerance while praising the holiness of Crashaw's life and the excellence of his poetry (see the extract on page 14).

As well as being a vehicle for public praise, elegies were used to express grief and to come to terms with it by repeating the Christian message that death was the gateway to eternal life and, therefore, a cause for gladness whatever the initial distress of the mourner. Just such a working out of emotion and religious faith can be seen in the calm conclusion of Henry King's 'Exequy' for his first wife (lines 81–90, 115–120):

> Sleep on my love in thy cold bed
> Never to be disquieted!
> My last good night! Thou wilt not wake
> Till I thy fate shall overtake:
> Till age, or grief, or sickness must
> Marry my body to that dust
> It so much loves; and fill the room
> My heart keeps empty in thy tomb.
> Stay for me there; I will not fail to
> To meet thee in that hollow vale.
> …
> The thought of this bids me go on,
> And wait my dissolutïon
> With hope and comfort. Dear (forgive
> The crime) I am content to live
> Divided, with but half a heart,
> Till we shall meet and never part.

**Till I thy fate shall overtake**  until I die as well
**that hollow vale**  'the valley of the shadow of death' (Psalm 23)
**dissolutïon**  death

One poet whose elegies make very clear the significance of death is Vaughan. In the elegy 'They Are All Gone into the World of Light', not only does he think of those he mourns as having 'gone into the world of light', but he sees death as 'the jewel of the just' (Part 3, page 95–96).

## Religious faith: struggle and fear

Fears of judgement after death leading to damnation feature strongly in some of Donne's poems. In his sermons, Donne made it clear that he did not believe that souls were predestined by God to be sinners and therefore to go to hell, but he believed, nevertheless, that it was impossible to repent without God first giving the sinner grace to do so: 'Yet grace, if thou repent, thou canst not lack; / But who shall give thee that grace to begin?' (Divine Sonnet 4). It is this fear that God may not give him the grace to repent that lies behind a poem such as 'Batter my Heart',

Grace is available to all who are sincere — Donne is doubting himself

discussed on pages 39–41. The intensity of the language suggests an anxiety far greater than that revealed, for example, by Ben Jonson in 'A Hymn to God the Father', which finishes on a confident note:

> But I'll come in,
>   Before my loss
>   Me farther toss,
> As sure to win
>   Under his cross.

It is only in one or two of his poems, such as 'A Hymn to God my God, in my Sickness', that Donne addresses God with Jonson's confidence that he is 'sure to win'. In 'A Hymn to God the Father' (Part 3, page 72) he has first to address his final sin, which is a lack of confidence that God will save him ('a sin of fear'). It is only when that is forgiven that he can say: 'And having done that [forgiven my 'sin of fear'], thou hast done [you have finished / you have Donne], / I fear no more'.

George Herbert also writes of conflict, but puts it more in terms of his resentment at God's failure to respond to him, than his difficulty in repenting. Thus he asks indignantly in 'The Collar', 'Have I no harvest but a thorn / To let me blood?' in a way that could be taken not only to suggest the barrenness of his religious experience, but also to equate his suffering almost blasphemously with that of Christ crowned with thorns.

▶ Compare the use of the dramatic present tense in 'Batter my heart' with the use of the narrative past here at the end of 'The Collar' (below). What do the endings of the two poems suggest about the differences in the way in which the two poets see their relationship with God?

> But as I raved and grew more fierce and wild
>     At every word,
> Me thoughts I heard one calling, *Child:*
>     And I replied, *My Lord.*

In the introduction to *Silex Scintillans,* Henry Vaughan gratefully acknowledges the influence of 'the blessed man, Mr George Herbert, whose holy life and verse gained many pious converts (of whom I am the least [important])' and praises him for striving for 'perfection and true holiness' rather than 'wit'. Nevertheless, although Vaughan takes up many of Herbert's themes, his poems have their own distinctive quality. This is partly because he was writing after the Civil Wars when the Church that Herbert had loved had been suppressed, but it also reflects amongst other things Vaughan's sensitivity to the beauty of nature and his belief that God was to be found within and through nature.

In 'The Flower' (lines 8–14) Herbert writes of his recovery from a sense of separation from God in these terms:

> Who would have thought my shrivelled heart
> Could have recovered greenness? It was gone
>   Quite under ground; as flowers depart
> To see their mother-root, when they have blown;
>       Where they together
>       All the hard weather,
>   Dead to the world, keep house unknown.

**blown** blossomed

Vaughan takes up Herbert's image of the plant that has 'gone / Quite under ground' in 'I Walked the Other Day', but adapts it to write about the death of someone dear to him (probably his brother William). He describes how he went to look for a flower which was no longer there because it was winter (an image of death). Not satisfied with this, he began to dig for the bulb of the flower (lines 18–35):

>         And by and by
> I saw the warm recluse alone to lie
>       Where fresh and green
>   He lived of us unseen.
>
> Many a question intricate and rare
>       Did I there strow,
> But all I could extort was, that he now
>       Did there repair
> Such losses as befell him in this air
>       And would ere long
>   Come forth most fair and young.
>
> This passed, I threw the clothes quite o'er his head,
>       And stung with fear
> Of my own frailty dropped down many a tear
>       Upon his bed,
> Then sighing whispered, Happy are the dead!
>       What peace doth now
>   Rock him asleep below?

**recluse** someone who has chosen to live apart; in other words, the bulb
**strow** ask; literally, scatter
**befell him in this air** happened to him in the air above while alive

**Come forth most fair and young** a new flower in spring; resurrection to life in heaven
**clothes quite o'er his head** earth on the bulb; bed or grave clothes on the body

▶ Examine the ways in which Vaughan adapts and develops Herbert's image.

## Devotional techniques

Both Roman Catholics and Protestants were clear that devotional thoughts and
emotions could not just be left to chance, since otherwise the mind, lacking the
discipline of a structured approach, would be distracted, as Herbert's is in 'Denial':
'My bent thoughts, like a brittle bow, / Did fly asunder'.

A common technique was meditation. There were many variations in approach,
but at the heart of them all is a harnessing of mind and imagination. Typically, a
scene is imagined in great detail to bring to life perhaps an incident from the Bible, *→ Good*
especially the life of Christ, or something like the terror of Judgement Day. This *Friday*
scene is used to stimulate a fuller understanding of a religious truth and how it
affects the person meditating. As a result of this understanding, speakers then use
their willpower to summon up an emotion such as love of God or distress at sin
that will help them to be better Christians. Thus in the sonnet 'At the Round Earth's
Imagined Corners', Donne begins by imagining the Day of Judgement, but this
leads him to think how he will be judged for his sins and of his need to repent and
be forgiven (lines 9–12):

> But let them sleep, Lord, and me mourn a space,
> For, if above all these, my sins abound,
> 'Tis late to ask abundance of thy grace,
> When we are there.
>
> **them** the resurrected summoned to judgement
> **there** in front of the judgement throne

Devotion implies a commitment to a relationship, and Christian devotional poetry
is centred on a relationship with God that is expressed in prayer and praise.
Nevertheless, just as love poetry often focuses as much on the lover as the beloved,
so in religious poetry the reader is often as much aware of the sinner or worshipper
as of the God who is being asked for forgiveness or being worshipped. Donne's
focus on his own emotions whether as a lover of a woman or of God illustrates this
well. It is in hymns of praise that the poet's own personality is least apparent and
this is particularly the case in Crashaw's poems.

Even when Crashaw's meditations do refer to his own condition, they are quite
different in emphasis from Donne's poems, the quiet confidence meaning that the
poet's personality is very much in the background. For example, in lines 93–108
from 'The Flaming Heart', a meditation on the mystical saint, St Teresa

*Perhaps particularly as the voice is the sinner's*
*(Compare Love III from IGCSE where*
*Herbert offers God's voice as well as his own)*

(1515–1582), the intense poetic energy is focused on the saint's virtues. There is only a brief and quiet acknowledgement in the last three lines of the poet's own need to die for his sins and let Christ live in him, as he follows her example:

> O thou undaunted daughter of desires!
> By all thy dower of lights and fires;
> By all the eagle in thee, all the dove;
> By all thy lives and deaths of love;
> By thy large draughts of intellectual day,
> And by thy thirst of love more large than they;
> By all thy brim-filled bowls of fierce desire;
> By thy last morning's draught of liquid fire;
> By the full kingdom of that final kiss
> That seized thy parting soul, and sealed thee his;
> By all the heavens thou hast in him
> (Fair sister of the SERAPHIM!);
> By all of HIM we have in THEE;
> Leave nothing of my SELF in me.
> Let me so read thy life, that I
> Unto all life of mine may die.

**Seraphim**  one of the categories of angels

## Links between the imagery of love and religious poetry

The links between the feelings expressed in religious poetry and in love poetry may seem surprising, but they are often closely related. For example, Donne has a fear of rejection in love that is not all that different from the fear of rejection by God expressed in 'Batter my Heart'. In 'Love's Deity' (lines 22–28) he finds himself in an impossible situation in which the only thing worse than loving a woman who does not love him would be to stop loving her, or for her to love him, thus proving herself unfaithful to her present lover:

> Rebel and atheist too, why murmur I,
>   As though I felt the worst that love could do?
> Love might make me leave loving, or might try
>   A deeper plague, to make her love me too,
> Which, since she loves before, I am loth to see;
> Falsehood is worse than hate; and that must be,
>   If she whom I love, should love me.

**atheist**  not believing the religion of love
**leave**  stop

**loves before** already loves another
**loth** reluctant

In other poems, it seems that Donne chooses religious ideas and images because they have the emotional force that he needs to express his feelings. Consider for example this passage from the opening of 'Twicknam Garden' (lines 5–9) in which he moves rapidly through a series of such images:

> But O, self traitor, I do bring
> The spider love, which transubstantiates all,
>   And can convert manna to gall,
> And that this place may thoroughly be thought
>   True paradise, I have the serpent brought.

Warped human love has the reverse effect of divine love, causing a transubstantiation not of bread and wine into Christ's body and blood (see page 19), but of something good, represented by 'manna', the life-saving food that God provided the Jews in the desert, into 'gall', a bitter tasting substance associated with the crucifixion, but also suggesting a sore caused by repeated rubbing. Then Donne goes on to suggest ironically that the place must be 'true paradise' since he has brought with him the serpent that will corrupt it.

Just as religious imagery gives force to expressions of love for other humans, so equally images of sexual love, including Petrarchan ones, are used to express religious love. This may seem surprising, but is easier to understand if you bear in mind that the soul is normally referred to as 'she' regardless of the sex of the body, and that it was customary to interpret the distinctly erotic love songs of *The Song of Solomon* in the Old Testament as showing the love between Christ and the Church (the Church is sometimes referred to as the 'Bride of Christ'). A striking example of treating the language of *The Song of Solomon* in a way that is also Petrarchan is found in this description of Christ after his resurrection. The extract is from lines 1313–1320 of *Salve Deus Rex Iudaeorum* ('Hail God, King of the Jews') by Aemilia Lanyer, a contemporary of Donne:

> Black as a raven in her blackest hue;
> His lips like scarlet threads, yet much more sweet
> Than is the sweetest honey dropping dew,
> Or honey combs, where all the bees do meet;
> Yea, he is constant, and his words are true,
> His cheeks are beds of spices, flowers sweet;
>   His lips, like lilies, dropping down pure myrrh,
>   Whose love, before all worlds we do prefer.

There is nothing like this in Donne. Just as he only uses Petrarchan conventions in a subversive way in his love poetry, so he only uses them in an unconventional way in his religious poems. For example, when he uses the traditional imagery of the Church as the bride of Christ in 'Show me dear Christ, thy spouse, so bright and clear', a poem about finding the true Church, he finishes with the disconcerting paradox that the true Church /faithful 'spouse' (bride) is the one that is like a sexually promiscuous wife, and freely available to men:

> Betray kind husband [Christ] thy spouse to our sights,
> And let mine amorous soul court thy mild dove,
> Who is most true, and pleasing to thee, then
> When she's embraced and open to most men.

Where he does use the Petrarchan images of floods of tears and burning, as in 'I Am a Little World' (lines 7–14), the tears are tears of repentance for sins and the flames are not of love, but of lust that has to be burnt away by the flames of purifying fire:

> Pour new seas in mine eyes, that so I might
> Drown my world with my weeping earnestly,
> Or wash it if it must be drowned no more:
> But oh it must be burnt; alas the fire
> Of lust and envy have burnt it heretofore,
> And made it fouler; let their flames retire,
> And burn me O Lord, with a fiery zeal
> Of thee and thy house, which doth in eating heal.

eating  consuming in flames

Of all the metaphysical poets, it is Crashaw, influenced by the writings of mystics such as St Teresa and St John of the Cross, who sees God as a lover and the soul as a bride. Consequently he adapts Petrarchan love imagery to express his love of God. In writing about St Teresa, Crashaw is influenced by her description of the mystical vision of love's dart in which an angel appeared and plunged a burning golden dart into her causing her unspeakable joys. This blending of Cupid's arrows with the spear that was thrust into Christ's side appealed strongly to Crashaw. In 'The Flaming Heart' (lines 68–70), he writes about a picture of this vision and tells the painter that as long as he paints Teresa with the flaming heart, he will have given her the means to plant a whole quiver of love's arrows in all those inspired by her example:

> Leave her alone the flaming heart.
>   Leave her that; and thou shalt leave her
> Not one loose shaft but love's whole quiver.

METAPHYSICAL POETRY

Thus the Petrarchan image of the heart wounded by love's arrow is turned into a source of further darts that will enflame more hearts with the love of God.

## Emblem books

Emblem books were a way of popularising religious ideas through engravings of symbolic pictures. Each was accompanied by a biblical quotation and a short poem explaining the picture's significance, followed by a four-line epigram summing up the message. The title page of *Silex Scintillans* has just such a picture (reproduced on the front cover of this book). Opposite it is a poem in Latin explaining how Vaughan's heart was as hard as a flint and unreceptive to God's influence until God struck him. This is probably a reference to the death of his younger brother William – and perhaps also to the execution of Charles I and the suppression of the Church of England. God struck fire from Vaughan's flinty heart (the flames of devotion go up towards God), but at the same time turned it to flesh so that Vaughan became capable of feeling grief for his sins, hence the falling tears. At the same time a new man emerges and can be seen looking from the heart. The use of emblems in this way to tease out a complex of meanings from an initial image encourages a search for analogies and symbolism, which is typical of the metaphysical style generally and the conceit in particular.

Vaughan's word painting of a waterfall in 'The Waterfall' and Marvell's of a drop of dew in 'On a Drop of Dew' are examples of poems which imitate the verses that accompanied emblems. They also aim to appeal to the reader's imagination in order to convey a message.

## Pastoral: withdrawal into the countryside

'A Dialogue between Thyrsis and Dorinda' by Andrew Marvell immediately makes clear that the poetry of pastoral retreat is not mere escapism, for this poem is set in the real world in which the enclosure of common land by landowners was causing great hardship. It is true that Thyrsis does tell Dorinda about an ideal pastoral environment (lines 33–34):

> There birds sing consorts, garlands grow,
> Cool winds do whisper, springs do flow.
>
> **consorts** harmonious songs

– but it only exists in the next world ('Elyzium'). It is also so much more attractive than the harsh world in which they actually live, that Dorinda proposes that they commit suicide in order to reach it. In other words, the only pastoral ideal offered in this poem is acknowledged to be a fantasy. The only escapism on offer is a

Next 2 pages about Pastoral–

suicide which is made possible by soaking the pastorally attractive poppies in wine to extract the opium.

If this is a sobering view of pastoral, Marvell's 'The Garden' does seem to offer a refuge: 'Fair quiet! Have I found thee here, / And Innocence, thy sister dear!' The visionary nature of the quiet found where the mind 'Withdraws into its happiness' and 'creates ... Far other worlds, and other seas, / Annihilating all that's made / To a green thought in a green shade' is not unlike that in many of Traherne's poems. As so often, both in Marvell's poetry and in pastoral, the question that then has to be asked is whether what has been said should be taken at face value. Having established that this is a garden of solitude, rather than a garden of love, and that it is solitude which makes possible the mind's ecstatic withdrawal from the body, Marvell then writes (lines 57–64):

> Such was the happy garden-state,
> While man there walked without a mate:
> After a place so pure, and sweet,
> What other help could yet be meet!
> But 'twas beyond a mortal's share
> To wander solitary there:
> Two paradises 'twere in one
> To live in paradise alone.

**meet** appropriate; Eve is described as a 'help meet' for Adam in the *Authorised Version*
**Two paradises 'twere** it would be two paradises

▶ Does the claim made here fit into the overall reasoning of the poem? What effect does the tone have on your reading of the poem? Compare the tone here with that of other pastoral poems that you have read.

The 'country house' poem looks at the countryside in a different way. It celebrates the benefits which derive from the order and control brought by a great landowner to his estate and tenants, as epitomised in his house. It also praises his personal virtues. Thus in 'To Penshurst', Ben Jonson's opening not only describes the house, but also implies the modesty of its owner, Sir Robert Sidney:

> Thou art not, Penshurst, built to envious show,
>   Of touch, or marble; nor canst boast a row
> Of polished pillars, or a roof of gold:
>   Thou hast no lantern, whereof tales are told.

**touch** black marble
**lantern** glazed structure at top of house to let in light

In 'Upon Appleton House, To my Lord Fairfax' Marvell appears at first to follow the same pattern – he was Fairfax's employee and might reasonably be expected to compliment his patron (lines 33–38, 41–42):

And surely when the after age
Shall hither come in pilgrimage,
These sacred places to adore,
By Vere and Fairfax trod before,
Men will dispute how their extent
Within such dwarfish confines went:
...
Humility alone designs
Those short but admirable lines ...

**how their extent**   how people of such importance

This praise of Fairfax's modesty, however, is set against the knowledge that he resigned as commander-in-chief of the Parliamentary army rather than lead it against the Scots, leaving the task to Cromwell. Regret for the sufferings of war and the Civil Wars is both stated explicitly and implied, but the question remains as to whether Marvell's praise of Fairfax is unconditional or whether it implies that he should have done more (lines 345–349, 353–354):

And yet there walks one on the sod
Who, had it pleasèd him and God,
Might once have made our gardens spring
Fresh as his own and flourishing.
But ...
...
... he did, with his utmost skill,
Ambition weed, but conscience till.

**our gardens**   the whole nation's gardens

It seems difficult not to read in this poem an echo of the 'Horatian Ode' as a criticism of Fairfax's withdrawal from public life. In the 'Horatian Ode' Marvell had written: 'So restless Cromwell could not cease / In the inglorious arts of peace'. In 'Upon Appleton House' he wrote of Fairfax: 'Who when retirèd here to peace / His warlike studies could not cease'. It emerges, however, that the 'warlike studies' consist of arranging flowerbeds to look like a fort and not tending the 'garden' of the country as a whole.

# War and public affairs

Among the earlier metaphysical poets, evidence of engagement in public life is
found primarily in Donne's writings. Reference has already been made to his
accounts of the expedition made under Essex in 1597. If his epigram 'A Burnt Ship'
shows little sensitivity ('So all were lost, which in the ship were found, / They in the
sea being burnt, they in the burnt ship drowned'), it does show realism alongside
the desire to be witty. A similar realism is apparent in his verse letter ('H.W. in
Hibernia Belligeranti', lines 9–12) to Sir Henry Wotton while he was taking part in
Essex's badly managed campaign in Ireland in 1599:

> Let shot, and bogs, and skeins
> With bodies deal, as fate bids or restrains;
> Ere sicknesses attack, young death is best,
> Who pays before his death doth 'scape arrest.

**skeins** Irish daggers
**Ere** before
**'scape** escape

The most direct comment on public affairs is made in satire. Donne's satires are
concerned with the general state of society, and are made more lively by accounts
of imagined meetings about town, which are embellished with appropriate dialogue
as in this extract from Satire 1 (lines 83–90):

> Now leaps he upright, jogs me, and cries, 'Do you see
> Yonder well-favoured youth?' 'Which?' 'Oh, 'tis he
> That dances so divinely'; 'Oh,' said I,
> 'Stand still, must you dance here for company?'
> He drooped, we went, till one (which did excel
> The Indians, in drinking his tobacco well)
> Met us; they talked; I whispered, 'Let us go,
> It may be you smell him not, truly I do.'

**well-favoured** handsome
**drinking** inhaling

The exception is Satire 3 which, although starting in typical satire style, focuses on
the specific issue of how a Christian should choose the right Church. This satire
has an earnest energy which reminds us that this was a key personal issue for
Donne himself (lines 79–85):

*Look for this poem—*
*It is very useful on*
*Donne's faith*

On a huge hill,
Cragged, and steep, Truth stands, and he that will

*(Context*
*conflict within*
*Christian Faith —*

Reach her, about must, and about must go;
And what the hill's suddenness resists, win so;
Yet strive so, that before age, death's twilight,
Thy soul rest, for none can work in that night;
To will, implies delay, therefore now do.

*Roman Catholics —*
*Protestants — Calvinists*
*Church of England —*

**suddenness** steepness
**that night** the 'night' of death

*Donne concludes - look to God only )*

**To will, implies delay** to intend to act means that you are not yet doing so

Marvell's satire is very different in style. As a politician he had detailed knowledge of the scandals and political manoeuvrings of the 1660s and he does not hesitate to make personal attacks to support his criticism of the government's handling of affairs. What both satirists have in common is a willingness to be unpleasant in order to make their points. Marvell, whose viewpoint is so difficult to establish in his other poems, has no compunction in his poem 'The Last Instructions to a Painter' (lines 81–82), in holding up to mockery the King's mistress's infatuation with a servant:

She through her lackey's drawers, as he ran,
Discerned love's cause and a new flame began.

**flame** passionate affair

However, his purpose is not to enjoy obscenity for its own sake, but to illustrate the corruption and dishonour which is found not only in the private lives of the court supporters, but also in their manipulation of Parliament.

Poetry like this may seem a long way from what is normally thought of as metaphysical. It is, however, a reminder that the metaphysical poets would not have recognised the name that we give them, and that they were willing to engage in poetry with every aspect of their experience.

## Assignments

1   Read the extract from Joseph Hall's satire on the writers of Petrarchan love poetry (Part 3, page 73). Is it possible to read any of Donne's love poems as responses to the attitude shown by Hall in this poem? In what ways does Hall's attitude to women differ from Donne's?

2   Compare Donne's 'The Ecstasy' with two or three of his other love poems. How far can 'The Ecstasy', or the other poems you have chosen, be said to be truly 'platonic' in their treatment of love?

3   Can you deduce anything about the woman's response in Donne's 'Sweetest Love, I Do Not Go' (Part 3, page 69)? What is your reaction to the absence of the woman's voice?
    Read Wroth's 'Sweetest Love Return Again' (Part 3, page 97) and compare it to Donne's poem. In what ways can Wroth's poem be seen as a reply to Donne's?

4   Compare the emotions revealed by Donne's use of religious imagery in his love poems and by his use of love imagery in his religious poems.

5   Compare Herrick's 'To His Angry God' with Herbert's 'The Collar' (Part 3, page 79 and page 76). There are certain similarities in the imagery: do you find therefore that the poems are similar in mood all the way through? Give your reasons.

6   Ben Jonson's 'An Epistle to a Friend, to Persuade Him to the Wars' ((Part 3, page 80) may have been written in about 1620 to persuade someone called Colby to volunteer to fight abroad in support of the leader of the German Protestants, Frederick, the Elector Palatine. Compare Jonson's treatment of war with those revealed in Donne's letter to Sir Henry Wotton and Marvell's 'Horatian Ode' (Part 3, page 85).

# Texts and extracts

This part provides material for comparison and to illustrate the ideas discussed elsewhere in the book. The poems are listed by alphabetical order of poet and the one prose extract is placed at the end. The spellings of the poems have been modernised, but the punctuation has not been altered except where it is misleading, since it gives some clue as to how the verse might have been read. The two syllables of the word-ending '-tion' are shown as '-tiön'; where the ending '-ed' is a separate syllable it is shown as '-èd'.

## Thomas Carew (1595–1640)

Carew's elegy on Donne sums up the opinions of Donne's admirers at the time of his death.

### from 'An Elegy upon the Death of Doctor Donne, Dean of St Paul's'

The Muses' garden, with pedantic weeds[1]
O'er-spread, was purged by thee, the lazy seeds
Of servile[2] imitation thrown away,
And fresh invention[3] planted;
...
Thou hast ... opened us a mine[4]
Of rich and pregnant fancy, drawn a line
Of masculine expression, ...
...
Thou shalt yield no precedence, but of time[5],
And the blind fate of language, whose tuned chime
More charms the outward sense; yet thou may'st claim
From so great disadvantage, greater fame,
Since to the awe of thy imperious wit[6]
Our troublesome language bends, made only fit
With her tough thick-ribbed hoops, to gird about
Thy giant fancy, which had proved too stout[7]
For their soft melting phrases.
...
Though every pen should share a distinct part,
Yet art thou theme[8] enough to tire all art;
Let others carve the rest; it shall suffice,
I on thy grave this epitaph incise.
*Here lies a King, that ruled as he thought fit*
*The universal monarchy of wit,*
*Here lie two flamens[9], and both those the best,*
*Apollo's first[10], at last the true God's priest.*

1 The Muses' garden, with pedantic weeds / O'er-spread, was purged by
  **thee** you weeded out from the garden of poetry dry, academic images and language
2 **servile** slavish
3 **invention** the finding of appropriate subject matter
4 **mine** the mine of 'golden' expression referred to later in the poem
5 **Thou shalt yield no precedence, but of time** earlier poets are older, but not better than you
6 **the awe of thy imperious wit** the awesomeness of your commanding wit
7 **too stout** too strong and unyielding
8 **theme** subject matter
9 **flamens** priests in the service of a particular god
10 **Apollo's first** first the priest of Apollo, the god of poetry

## John Donne (1572–1631)

### 'The Ecstasy'

Where, like a pillow on a bed,
  A pregnant bank swelled up, to rest
The violet's reclining head,
  Sat we two, one another's best;

Our hands were firmly cemented
  With a fast balm, which thence did spring,
Our eye-beams twisted, and did thread
  Our eyes, upon one double string;

So to intergraft our hands, as yet
  Was all our means to make us one,
And pictures in our eyes¹ to get²
  Was all our propagatiön.

As 'twixt two equal armies, Fate
  Suspends uncertain victory,
Our souls (which to advance their state³,
  Were gone out) hung 'twixt her, and me.

And whilst our souls negotiate there,
  We like sepulchral statues lay;
All day, the same our postures were,
  And we said nothing, all the day.

If any, so by love refined,
  That he soul's language understood,
And by good love were grown all mind,
  Within convenient distance stood,

He (though he knew not which soul spake
  Because both meant, both spake the same)
Might thence a new concoction[4] take,
  And part far purer than he came.

This ecstasy doth unperplex
  (We said) and tell us what we love,
We see by this, it was not sex,
  We see, we saw not what did move[5]:

But as all several souls contain
  Mixture of things, they know not what,
Love, these mixed souls doth mix again,
  And makes both one, each this and that.

A single violet transplant,
  The strength, the colour, and the size
(All which before was poor, and scant)
  Redoubles still, and multiplies.

When love, with one another so
  Interinanimates[6] two souls,
That abler soul, which thence doth flow[7],
  Defects of loneliness controls.

We then, who are this new soul, know,
  Of what we are composed, and made,
For, the atomies[8] of which we grow,
  Are souls, whom no change can invade.

But O alas, so long, so far
  Our bodies why do we forbear[9]?
They are ours, though they are not we: we are
  The intelligences[10], they the sphere.

We owe them thanks, because they thus
  Did us, to us, at first convey,
Yielded their forces, sense, to us,
  Nor are dross to us, but allay[11].

On man heaven's influence works not so,
  But that it first imprints the air[12],
So soul into the soul may flow,
  Though it to body first repair[13].

As our blood labours to beget[14]
  Spirits[15], as like souls as it can,
Because such fingers need to knit
  That subtle knot, which makes us man[16]:

So must pure lovers' souls descend
  To affections, and to faculties[17],
Which sense may reach and apprehend,
  Else a great prince in prison lies[18].

To our bodies turn we then, that so
  Weak men on love revealed may look;
Love's mysteries in souls do grow,
  But yet the body is his book.

And if some lover, such as we,
  Have heard this dialogue of one,
Let him still mark[19] us, he shall see
  Small change, when we're to bodies gone.

---

[1] **pictures in our eyes**  reflections of each other

[2] **get**  beget/conceive

[3] **advance their state**  promote their cause

[4] **concoction**  purification by heating – an alchemical term

[5] **we saw not what did move**  we did not understand what made us love

[6] **Interinanimates**  the souls give life to each other

[7] **That abler soul, which thence doth flow**  the new soul derived from the other two

[8] **atomies**  component parts

[9] **forbear**  refrain from using

[10] **intelligences**  heavenly spheres are controlled by an intelligence or angel, just as the bodies are controlled by souls

[11] **Nor are dross ... but allay**  not the scum on top of molten ore, but a (useful) alloy

[12] **imprints the air**  angels become visible by taking a body made of air

[13] **repair**  go

[14] **labours to beget**  works to create

[15] **Spirits**  vapours thought to link mind and body

[16] **That subtle knot, which makes us man**  the link of body and mind that makes us alive

[17] **affections, and to faculties**  feelings and physical powers

[18] **Else a great prince in prison lies**  like the soul, a prince must act through agents or be helpless

[19] **mark**  observe

### 'Song'

Sweetest love, I do not go,
   For weariness of thee,
Nor in hope the world can show
   A fitter love for me;
      But since that I
Must die at last, 'tis best,
To use my self in jest
   Thus by feigned[1] deaths to die.

Yesternight the sun went hence,
   And yet is here today;
He hath no desire nor sense[2],
   Nor half so short a way:
      Then fear not me,
But believe that I shall make
Speedier journeys, since I take
   More wings and spurs than he.

O how feeble is man's power,
   That if good fortune fall,
Cannot add another hour,
   Nor a lost hour recall!
      But come bad chance,
And we join to it our strength,
And we teach it art and length,
   Itself o'er us to advance.

When thou sigh'st, thou sigh'st not wind,
   But sigh'st my soul away,
When thou weep'st, unkindly kind,
   My life's blood doth decay[3].
      It cannot be
That thou lov'st me, as thou say'st,
If in thine my life thou waste;
   Thou art the best of me.

Let not thy divining heart
   Forethink[4] me any ill,
Destiny may take thy part,
   And may thy fears fulfil;
      But think that we
Are but turned aside to sleep;
They who one another keep
   Alive[5], ne'er parted be.

---

[1] **feigned**  pretended
[2] **He hath no desire nor sense**  the sun is
   inanimate
[3] **When thou sigh'st … / My life's blood
   doth decay**  because the pair are so
   united, her distress causes his spiritual
   and physical decay

[4] **Forethink**  imagine in advance
[5] **They who one another keep / Alive**  They
   possess each other's hearts

---

### 'A Valediction: Forbidding Mourning'

As virtuous men pass mildly away,
   And whisper to their souls, to go,
Whilst some of their sad friends do say,
   The breath goes now[1], and some say, no:

So let us melt, and make no noise,
   No tear-floods, nor sigh-tempests move,
'Twere profanation[2] of our joys
   To tell the laity[3] our love.

Moving of the earth brings harms and fears,
   Men reckon what it did and meant,
But trepidation[4] of the spheres,
   Though greater far, is innocent[5].

Dull sublunary[6] lovers' love
   (Whose soul is sense) cannot admit
Absence, because it doth remove
   Those things which elemented it[7].

But we by a love, so much refined,
   That our selves know not what it is,
Inter-assurèd of the mind,
   Care less, eyes, lips, and hands to miss.

Our two souls therefore, which are one,
   Though I must go, endure not yet
A breach, but an expansiön,
   Like gold to aery thinness beat.

If they be two, they are two so
   As stiff twin compasses are two,
Thy soul the fixed foot, makes no show
   To move, but doth, if the other do.

And though it in the centre sit,
   Yet when the other far doth roam,
It leans, and hearkens after it,
   And grows erect, as that comes home.

Such wilt thou be to me, who must
   Like the other foot, obliquely run;
Thy firmness makes my circle just,
   And makes me end, where I begun.

---

[1] **The breath goes now** he has now stopped breathing

[2] **profanation** desecration

[3] **the laity** those who are not priests of love

[4] **trepidation** a movement of one of the heavenly spheres

[5] **innocent** harmless

[6] **sublunary** beneath the sphere of the moon and subject to decay

[7] **(Whose soul is sense)... elemented it** whose love depends on physical contact, cannot cope with absence, because it removes the elements from which love is made

### 'A Hymn to God the Father'

Wilt thou forgive that sin where I begun[1],
    Which was my sin, though it were done before?
Wilt thou forgive that sin, through which I run,
    And do run still: though still I do deplore[2]?
        When thou hast done, thou hast not done,
           For, I have more[3].

Wilt thou forgive that sin which I have won[4]
    Others to sin? and, made my sin their door?[5]
Wilt thou forgive that sin which I did shun
    A year, or two: but wallowed in, a score?
        When thou hast done, thou hast not done,
           For, I have more.

I have a sin of fear, that when I have spun
    My last thread[6], I shall perish on the shore[7];
But swear by thy self, that at my death thy Sun[8]
    Shall shine as he shines now, and heretofore;
        And, having done that, thou hast done[9],
           I fear no more.

---

[1] **that sin where I begun** original sin (see page 18)

[2] **though still I do deplore** although I still greatly regret it

[3] **When thou hast done, … For, I have more** when you have forgiven it, you have not finished, because I have more sins

[4] **won** persuaded

[5] **their door** their entrance to sin

[6] **a sin of fear … have spun / My last thread** a sinful lack of faith … finished my earthly life

[7] **shore** the point between earth and heaven

[8] **thy Sun** Christ, the Son of God

[9] **thou hast done** you have finished / you have Donne

# Joseph Hall (1574–1656)

Joseph Hall's satires were amongst those banned in the 1590s. This extract shows a young man's contempt for the conventions of traditional Petrarchan love poetry at the time when Donne was probably writing some of his early love poems.

### from Virgidemiarum *Book 1, Satire 7*

The love-sick poet, whose importune prayer[1]
Repulsèd is with resolute despair,
Hopeth to conquer his disdainful dame,
With public plaints of his conceivèd[2] flame.
Then pours he forth in patchèd sonettings[3]
His love, his lust, and loathsome flatterings:
As though the staring world hanged on his sleeve[4],
When once he smiles to laugh: and when he sighs to grieve.
Careth the world, thou love, thou live, or die?
Careth the world, how fair thy fair one be?
Fond wit-old, that would'st load thy witless head
With timely horns, before thy bridal bed[5].
Then can he term his dirty ill-faced bride
Lady and Queen, and virgin deified[6]:
Be she all sooty-black, or berry-brown,
She's white as morrow's milk, or flakes[7] new blown.

---

[1] **importune prayer** irritatingly persistent advances
[2] **plaints of his conceivèd flame** lamentations of his imagined love
[3] **patchèd sonettings** derivative and poorly written love poems
[4] **hanged on his sleeve** was eager to know what he had to say
[5] **Fond wit-old … before thy bridal bed** fool who wants to wear horns – the sign of betrayal – even before marriage
[6] **deified** made a goddess
[7] **flakes** snow flakes

# George Herbert (1593–1633)

### 'Affliction (I)'

When first thou didst entice to thee my heart,
　　　　I thought the service brave[1]:
So many joys I writ down for my part,
　　　　Besides what I might have
Out of my stock of natural delights,
Augmented with thy gracious benefits.

I lookèd on thy furniture so fine,
　　　　And made it fine to me:
Thy glorious household-stuff did me entwine,
　　　　And 'tice[2] me unto thee.
Such stars I counted mine: both heaven and earth
Paid me my wages in a world of mirth.

What pleasures could I want, whose King I served?
　　　　Where joys my fellows were.
Thus argued into hopes, my thoughts reserved
　　　　No place for grief or fear.
Therefore my sudden soul caught at the place,
And made her youth and fierceness seek thy face.

At first thou gav'st me milk and sweetnesses;
　　　　I had my wish and way:
My days were strawed with[3] flowers and happiness;
　　　　There was no month but May.
But with my years sorrow did twist and grow,
And made a party[4] unawares for woe.

My flesh began unto my soul[5] in pain,
　　　　Sicknesses cleave my bones;
Consuming agues[6] dwell in every vein,
　　　　And tune my breath to groans.
Sorrow was all my soul; I scarce believed,
Till grief did tell me roundly[7], that I lived.

When I got health, thou took'st away my life,
　　　　And more; for my friends die:
My mirth and edge was lost; a blunted knife
　　　　Was of more use than I.
Thus thin and lean without a fence or friend,
I was blown through with every storm and wind.

Whereas my birth and spirit rather took
    The way that takes the town;
Thou didst betray me to a lingering book,
    And wrap me in a gown[8].
I was entangled in the world of strife,
Before I had the power to change my life.

Yet, for I threatened[9] oft the siege to raise,
    Not simpering all mine age,
Thou often didst with academic praise
    Melt and dissolve my rage.
I took thy sweetened pill, till I came where
I could not go away, nor persevere.

Yet lest perchance I should too happy be
    In my unhappiness,
Turning my purge to food, thou throwest me
    Into more sicknesses.
Thus doth thy power cross-bias me[10], not making
Thine own gift good, yet me from my ways taking.

Now I am here, what thou wilt do with me
    None of my books will show:
I read, and sigh, and wish I were a tree;
    For sure then I should grow
To fruit or shade: at least some bird would trust
Her household to me, and I should be just.

Yea, though thou troublest me, I must be meek;
    In weakness must be stout[11].
Well, I will change the service, and go seek
    Some other master out.
Ah my dear God! Though I am clean forgot,
Let[12] me not love thee, if I love thee not.

---

[1] **brave** attractive

[2] **'tice** entice; lure

[3] **strawed with** covered with

[4] **party** a conspiracy

[5] **began unto my soul** began to speak to my soul

[6] **agues** fevers

[7] **roundly** plainly

[8] **gown** the gown of a university don or priest

[9] **for I threatened** because I threatened

[10] **doth thy power cross-bias me** God's power is like the weight or bias in a bowl, making him change course

[11] **stout** brave

[12] **let** allow, or hinder

### 'The Collar'

I struck the board, and cried, No more.
            I will abroad.
What? Shall I ever sigh and pine?
My lines and life are free; free as the road,
    Loose as the wind, as large as store.
         Shall I be still in suit[1]?
Have I no harvest but a thorn
To let me blood, and not restore
What I have lost with cordial fruit[2]?
         Sure there was wine
Before my sighs did dry it: there was corn
    Before my tears did drown it.
  Is the year only lost to me?
       Have I no bays[3] to crown it?
No flowers, no garlands gay? All blasted?
       All wasted?
  Not so, my heart: but there is fruit,
      And thou hast hands.
  Recover all thy sigh-blown age
On double pleasures: leave thy cold dispute
Of what is fit, and not[4]. Forsake thy cage,
      Thy rope of sands[5],
Which petty thoughts have made, and  made to thee
  Good cable, to enforce and draw[6],
      And be thy law,
While thou didst wink[7] and wouldst not see.
     Away; take heed:
     I will abroad.
Call in thy death's head[8] there: tie up thy fears.
     He that forbears[9]
  To suit and serve his need[10],
     Deserves his load.
But as I raved and grew more fierce and wild
     At every word,
Me thoughts I heard one calling, *Child:*
    And I replied, *My Lord.*

---

[1] **still in suit** always begging
[2] **cordial fruit** restorative fruit
[3] **bays** a wreath of bay leaves for a
   conqueror or poet

[4] **what is fit, and not** what is morally right
  or not
[5] **rope of sands** i.e. it is not 'good cable'
[6] **to enforce and draw** pull you to do things
  that you don't want to

### 'Denial'

When my devotions could not pierce
     Thy silent ears;
Then was my heart broken, as was my verse:
   My breast was full of fears
     And disorder.

My bent thoughts, like a brittle bow,
     Did fly asunder:
Each took his way; some would to pleasures go,
   Some to the wars and thunder
     Of alarms.

As good go anywhere, they say,
     As to benumb
Both knees and heart, in crying night and day,
   *Come, come, my God, O come,*
     But no hearing.

O that thou should'st give dust[1] a tongue
     To cry to thee,
And then not hear it crying! all day long
   My heart was in my knee,
     But no hearing.

Therefore my soul lay out of sight,
     Untuned, unstrung:
My feeble spirit, unable to look right,
   Like a nipped blossom, hung
     Discontented.

O cheer and tune my heartless[2] breast,
     Defer no time;
That so thy favours granting my request,
   They and my mind may chime,
     And mend my rhyme.

### 'Easter'

Rise heart; thy Lord is risen. Sing his praise
                    Without delays,
Who takes thee by the hand, that thou likewise
                    With him mayst rise:
That, as his death calcinèd¹ thee to dust,
His life may make thee gold, and much more just.

Awake, my lute, and struggle for thy part
                    With all thy art.
The cross taught all wood to resound his name
                    Who bore the same².
His stretchèd sinews taught all strings³, what key
Is best to celebrate this most high day.

Consort⁴ both heart and lute, and twist a song
                    Pleasant and long:
Or since all music is but three parts vied
                    And multiplied;
O let thy blessèd Spirit bear a part⁵,
And make up our defects with his sweet art.

I got me flowers to straw thy way⁶;
I got me boughs off many a tree:
But thou wast up by break of day,
And brought'st thy sweets⁷ along with thee.

The sun arising in the East,
Though he give light and the East perfume;
If they should offer to contest
With thy arising, they presume⁸.

Can there be any day but this,
Though many suns to shine endeavour?
We count three hundred, but we miss⁹:
There is but one, and that one ever¹⁰.

<sup>1</sup> **calcinèd**  burned to ashes – an alchemical
 term
<sup>2</sup> **Who bore the same**  the cross carried
 Christ's body
<sup>3</sup> **stretchèd sinews taught all strings**
 Christ's sinews stretched on the cross
 are like the strings of the lute
<sup>4</sup> **Consort**  perform together

<sup>5</sup> **bear a part**  play one of the parts in the
 music
<sup>6</sup> **straw thy way**  spread in your path
<sup>7</sup> **sweets**  blossoms; goodness
<sup>8</sup> **they presume**  they are presumptuous
<sup>9</sup> **miss**  miss the point
<sup>10</sup> **There is but one, and that one ever**  not
 the sun, but the Son of God – Christ

---

# Robert Herrick (1591–1674)

Herrick was a great admirer of Ben Jonson's poetry. He became a clergyman and
was ejected from his parish by the Puritans. His attitude to God in 'To his Angry
God' provides points of comparison with Donne and Herbert.

### 'To His Angry God'

 Through all the night
 Thou dost me fright,
And hold'st mine eyes from sleeping;
 And day by day,
 My cup can say,
My wine is mixed with weeping.

 Thou dost my bread
 With ashes knead,
Each evening and each morrow:
 Mine eye and ear
 Do see, and hear
The coming in of sorrow.

 Thy scourge of steel
 (Aye me!) I feel,
Upon me beating ever:
 While my sick heart
 With dismal smart
Is disacquainted never.

Long, long, I'm sure,
  This can't endure;
But in short time 'twill please Thee,
  My gentle God,
  To burn the rod[1],
Or strike so as to ease me.

---

[1] **rod**  the cane, i.e. God's means of
   punishing him

---

# Ben Jonson (1572–1637)

Ben Jonson was an exact contemporary of Donne, but unlike any of the
metaphysicals, chose to make his living as a writer. His 'Epistle to a Friend' can be
compared in style with Donne's epistles and satires, and also with Marvell's
'Horatian Ode', in its treatment of justifiable reasons for war. Compare 'Begging
Another' with Donne's love poems.

### from 'An Epistle to a Friend, to Persuade Him to the Wars'

Wake, friend from forth thy lethargy: the drum
Beats brave, and loud in Europe, and bids come
All that dare rouse: or are not loth to quit[1]
Their vicious[2] ease, and be o'erwhelmed with it.
It is a call to keep the spirits alive
That gasp for action, and would yet revive
Man's buried honour, in his sleepy life:
Quickening dead Nature[3], to her noblest strife.
  …

Our delicacies are grown capital[4],
And even our sports are dangers! What we call
Friendship is now masked hatred! Justice fled,
And shamefastness[5] together! All laws dead
That kept man living! Pleasures only sought!
Honour and honesty, as poor things thought
As they are made! Pride, and stiff clownage[6] mixed
To make up greatness! And man's whole good fixed
In bravery, or gluttony, or coin,
All which he makes the servants of the groin[7],
Thither it flows.
  …

These[8] take, and now go seek thy peace in war;
Who falls for love of God[9], shall rise a star.

---

[1] **loth to quit**  reluctant to leave
[2] **vicious**  given over to vices
[3] **Quickening dead Nature**  bringing Nature
   back to life
[4] **Our delicacies are grown capital**  our
   indulgent pleasures have become fatal
[5] **shamefastness**  modesty; decency
[6] **stiff clownage**  uncompromising folly
[7] **the groin**  sexual appetite
[8] **These**  my good wishes
[9] **falls for love of God**  dies fighting for the
   Protestant cause

---

### 'Begging Another, on Colour of Mending the Former'

For love's sake, kiss me once again,
   I long, and should not beg in vain,
      Here's none to spy, or see;
         Why do you doubt, or stay?
   I'll taste as lightly as the bee,
That doth but touch his flower, and flies away.
   Once more, and (faith) I will be gone:
   Can he that loves, ask less than one?
      Nay, you may err in this,
         And all your bounty wrong[1]:
This could be called but half a kiss.
What we're but once to do, we should do long:
   I will but mend the last, and tell
   Where, how it would have relished well;
      Join lip to lip, and try:
         Each suck other's breath;
And whilst our tongues perplexèd lie,
Let who will[2] think us dead, or wish our death.

---

[1] **all your bounty wrong**  wrong all your
   generosity
[1] **who will**  whoever wants to

# Aemilia Lanyer (1569–1645)

The daughter of an Italian court musician, Aemilia Lanyer married Alfonso Lanyer, a court musician and soldier who, like Donne, took part in the Earl of Essex's expedition to the Azores. She appears to have been encouraged in her writing of *Salve Deus Rex Iudaeorum* (Hail God, King of the Jews) by the Countess of Cumberland, and the poem is prefaced by dedications to a whole series of intelligent and good women.

Lanyer has reached the point in the story of the trial of Jesus before his crucifixion when Pilate's wife tells him to spare Jesus. He, a man, ignores her correct advice. This leads Lanyer to reflect on the time when Eve gave the apple to Adam and caused the Fall. Even then, she argues, the woman was not so much at fault as the man, because of her inability to see through Satan. She gave the apple to Adam out of love, but he ate it because he thought it looked nice. He was more at fault because his powers were greater. This passage is obviously making a statement about the status of women and not just offering a commentary on the Bible story.

### *from* Salve Deus Rex Iudaeorum

And then to lay the fault on patience' back,
That we, poor women, must endure it all!
We know right well he [Adam] did discretion lack,
Being not persuaded thereunto[1] at all.
If Eve did err, it was for knowledge sake,
The fruit being fair persuaded him to fall:
   No subtle serpent's falsehood did betray him,
   If he would eat it, who had power to stay him[2]?

Not Eve, whose fault was only too much love,
Which made her give this present to her Dear,
That what she tasted, he likewise might prove[3],
Whereby his knowledge might become more clear:
He never sought her weakness to reprove,
With those sharp words, which he of God did hear:
   Yet men will boast of Knowledge, which he took
   From Eve's fair hand, as from a learnèd book[4].

---

[1] **not persuaded thereunto** not intellectually convinced to do it

[2] **stay him** stop him

[3] **prove** experience

[4] **Yet men will boast ... from a learnèd book** the apple came from the forbidden tree of the knowledge of good and evil

# Christopher Marlowe (1564–93)

Ovid's openly sexual love poetry provided an alternative model for Donne and his contemporaries to the poetry of Petrarch.

### from Ovid's *Elegies, Book 2, Elegy 10, lines 25–38*

Pleasure adds fuel to my lustful fire,
I pay them home with that they most desire.
Oft have I spent the night in wantonness,
And in the morn been lively n'er the less.
He's happy who love's mutual skirmish slays,
And to the gods for that death Ovid prays.
Let soldiers chase their enemies amain[1],
And with their blood eternal honour gain;
Let merchants seek wealth with perjurèd lips,
Being wracked, carouse the sea[2] tired by their ships;
But when I die, would I might droop with doing[3],
And in the midst thereof, set my soul going,
That at my funerals some may weeping cry,
'Even as he led his life, so did he die.'

---

[1] **amain**  as fast as they can
[2] **Being wracked, carouse the sea**  being wrecked, let them drink the sea
[3] **But when I die ... doing**  doing is sexual intercourse; die can also mean to have an orgasm

---

# Andrew Marvell (1621–1678)

### 'To His Coy Mistress'

Had we but world enough, and time,
This coyness[1], Lady, were no crime.
We would sit down, and think which way
To walk, and pass our long love's day.
Thou by the Indian Ganges' side
Shouldst rubies find: I by the tide
Of Humber would complain[2]. I would
Love you ten years before the flood[3]:
And you should, if you please, refuse
Till the conversion of the Jews[4].
My vegetable love should grow
Vaster than empires, and more slow.
An hundred years should go to praise

Thine eyes, and on thy forehead gaze.
Two hundred to adore each breast:
But thirty thousand to the rest.
An age at least to every part,
And the last age should show your heart:
For, Lady, you deserve this state⁵;
Nor would I love at lower rate⁶.
   But at my back I always hear
Time's wingèd chariot hurrying near:
And yonder all before us lie
Deserts of vast eternity.
Thy beauty shall no more be found;
Nor, in thy marble vault⁷, shall sound
My echoing song: then worms shall try
That long-preserved virginity:
And your quaint honour⁸ turn to dust;
And into ashes all my lust.
The grave's a fine and private place,
But none, I think, do there embrace.
   Now, therefore, while the youthful glew⁹
Sits on thy skin like morning dew,
And while thy willing soul transpires
At every pore with instant fires,
Now let us sport us while we may;
And now, like amorous birds of prey,
Rather at once our time devour,
Than languish in his slow-chapped¹⁰ power.
Let us roll all our strength, and all
Our sweetness, up into one ball:
And tear our pleasures with rough strife,
Thorough the iron gates of life.
Thus, though we cannot make our sun
Stand still, yet we will make him run¹¹.

---

¹**coyness** shyness
²**complain** express my grief
³**the flood** Noah's flood
⁴**Till the conversion of the Jews** i.e. for a very long time
⁵**state** ceremonious treatment
⁶**lower rate** lower cost
⁷**vault** burial vault

⁸**quaint honour** prim chastity
⁹**glew** glow; or glue-like sweat?
¹⁰**slow-chapped** slowly chewing
¹¹**... our sun / Stand still, yet we will make him run** if time cannot be halted, at least it can pass rapidly because they are enjoying themselves

### 'An Horatian Ode upon Cromwell's Return from Ireland'

The forward youth that would appear
Must now forsake his muses dear,
   Nor in the shadows sing
   His numbers languishing[1].
'Tis time to leave the books in dust,
And oil the unusèd armour's rust:
   Removing from the wall
   The corslet[2] of the hall.
So restless Cromwell could not cease
In the inglorious arts of peace,
   But through adventurous war
   Urgèd his active star[3].
And, like the three-forked lightning, first
Breaking the clouds where it was nursed,
   Did thorough his own side[4]
   His fiery way divide.
For 'tis all one to courage high
The emulous[5] or enemy:
   And with such to enclose[6]
   Is more than to oppose.
Then burning through the air he went,
And palaces and temples rent:
   And Caesar's[7] head at last
   Did through his laurels[8] blast.
'Tis madness to resist or blame
The force of angry Heaven's flame:
   And, if we would speak true,
   Much to the man is due,
Who, from his private gardens, where
He lived reservèd and austere,
   As if his highest plot
   To plant the bergamot[9],
Could by industrious valour climb
To ruin the great work of time,
   And cast the kingdom old
   Into another mould,
Though Justice against Fate complain,
And plead the ancient rights in vain:
   But those do hold or break
   As men are strong or weak.
Nature, that hateth emptiness[10],
Allows of penetration less[11]:

And therefore must make room
Where greater spirits come.
What field of all the Civil Wars,
Where his were not the deepest scars?
    And Hampton shows what part
    He had of wiser art,
Where, twining subtle fears with hope,
He wove a net of such a scope,
    That Charles himself might chase
    To Carisbrooke's narrow case[12/13]
That thence the royal actor borne[14]
The tragic scaffold might adorn:
    While round the armèd bands
    Did clap their bloody hands.
He nothing common did or mean
Upon that memorable scene:
    But with his keener eye
    The axe's edge did try[15]:
Nor called the gods with vulgar spite
To vindicate[16] his helpless right,
    But bowed his comely[17] head,
    Down, as upon a bed.
This was that memorable hour
Which first assured the forcèd power[18].
    So when they did design
    The Capitol's[19] first line,
A bleeding head where they begun,
Did fright the architects to run;
    And yet in that the State
    Foresaw its happy fate[20].
And now the Irish are ashamed
To see themselves in one year tamed:
    So much one man can do,
    That does both act and know.
They can affirm his praises best[21],
And have, though overcome, confessed
    How good he is, how just,
    And fit for highest trust:
Nor yet grown stiffer with command,
But still in the Republic's hand[22]:
    How fit he is to sway[23]
    That can so well obey.
He to the Commons'[24] feet presents

A kingdom, for his first year's rents:
   And, what he may, forbears[25]
   His fame, to make it theirs:
And has his sword and spoils ungirt[26]
To lay them at the public's skirt[27].
   So when the falcon high
   Falls heavy from the sky,
She, having killed, no more does search
But[28] on the next green bough to perch,
   Where, when he first does lure[29],
   The falconer has her sure.
What may not then our isle presume
While Victory his crest does plume?
   What may not others fear
   If thus he crowns each year?
A Caesar, he, ere long to Gaul[30],
To Italy an Hannibal[31],
   And to all states not free
   Shall climacteric be[32].
The Pict[33] no shelter now shall find
Within his party-coloured mind[34],
   But from this valour sad[35]
   Shrink underneath the plaid[36]:
Happy, if in the tufted brake[37]
The English hunter him mistake[38],
   Nor lay his hounds in near[39]
   The Caledonian deer[40].
But thou, the Wars' and Fortune's son,
March indefatigably on,
   And for the last effect[41]
   Still keep thy sword erect:
Besides the force it has to fright
The spirits of the shady night,
   The same arts that did gain
   A power, must it maintain[42].

---

[1] **numbers languishing**  sentimental poetry
[2] **corslet**  piece of armour covering the body
[3] **Urgèd his active star**  he was born under a
   star which destined him to be active
[4] **thorough his own side**  through the
   commanders of the Parliamentary army
[5] **emulous**  jealous rivals

[6] **enclose**  to contain and control
[7] **Caesar's**  Charles I
[8] **laurels**  the laurel wreath worn by a ruler
[9] **bergamot**  type of pear tree
[10] **Nature, that hateth emptiness**  Nature,
   which abhors a vacuum

<sup></sup>11 **Allows of penetration less** still less allows two things in the same space at the same time

12 **And Hampton shows what part ... To Carisbrooke's narrow case** Cromwell's cunning was supposed to have led to Charles escaping from Hampton only to be betrayed by the govenor of Carisbrooke Castle and imprisoned there instead

13 **narrow case** narrow confines

14 **thence... borne** taken from there

15 **try** test

16 **vindicate** to justify and defend

17 **comely** dignified (rather than beautiful)

18 **forcèd** established by force

19 **Capitol's** the temple of Jupiter on the Capitol in Rome

20 **Foresaw its happy fate** the discovery of the severed head was a good omen

21 **They can affirm his praises best** the Irish; there is no hint of the savagery of the campaign

22 **in the Republic's hand** obeying Parliament

23 **to sway** to command

24 **Commons'** the House of Commons; Parliament

25 **forbears** refrains from asserting his fame

26 **ungirt** laid aside

27 **skirt** feet

28 **no more does search / But** wants to do nothing but

29 **lure** tempt back a bird of prey

30 **A Caesar, he, ere long to Gaul** Caesar conquered Gaul

31 **To Italy an Hannibal** Hannibal defeated the Romans initially

32 **Shall climacteric be** shall introduce a new era

33 **The Pict** the people of Scotland; Pict means painted

34 **party-coloured mind** the Scots had many rival groups and factions

35 **sad** seriously committed

36 **plaid** tartan cloak, which is also parti-coloured

37 **tufted brake** clump of bushes

38 **him mistake** fail to recognise him

39 **lay his hounds in near** put his hounds on the scent

40 **Caledonian deer** the hunted Scots

41 **last effect** last achievement; in Virgil's epic, *The Aeneid*, Aeneas is told to draw his sword in the underworld to keep the spirits at bay, but when he wants to use the sword he is told that it cannot harm bodiless spirits.

42 **The same arts ... it maintain** the military skills needed to win power are also needed to retain it

# Katherine Philips (1632–1664)

### *'Friendship's Mysteries, To my Dearest Lucasia'*

Come, my Lucasia, since we see
    That miracles men's faith do move,
By wonder and by prodigy
    To the dull angry world let's prove
    There's a religion in our love.

For though we were designed to agree[1],
   That fate no liberty destroys[2],
But our election[3] is as free
   As angels, who with greedy[4] choice
   Are yet determined to their joys[5].

Our hearts are doubled by their loss[6],
   Here mixture is addition grown;
We both diffuse, and both engross[7],
   And we, whose minds are so much one,
   Never, yet ever, are alone.

We court our own captivity[8],
   Than thrones more great and innocent:
'Twere banishment to be set free,
   Since we wear fetters whose intent
   Not bondage is, but ornament.

Divided joys are tedious found,
   And griefs united easier grow:
We are ourselves but by rebound[9],
   And all our titles shuffled so,
   Both princes, and both subjects too.

Our hearts are mutual victims laid,
   While they (such power in friendship lies)
Are altars, priests, and offerings made:
   And each heart which thus kindly dies,
   Grows deathless by the sacrifice.

---

[1] **designed to agree**  destined to love
[2] **That fate no liberty destroys**  no freedom
  of choice will destroy our destined fate
[3] **election**  choice
[4] **greedy**  eager
[5] **yet determined to their joys**  can
  nevertheless only choose joys
[6] **Our hearts are doubled by their
  loss**  they lose their hearts to each
  other, and paradoxically have two not
  one

[7] **diffuse, and both engross**  scatter and
  gather together
[8] **court our own captivity**  try to win the
  favour of being captive to each other
[9] **We are ourselves but by rebound**  we are
  only fully ourselves in responding to
  each other

## 'To my Excellent Lucasia, on our Friendship'

I did not live until this time
   Crowned my felicity,
When I could say without a crime,
   I am not thine, but thee.

This carcase breathed, and walked, and slept,
   So that the world believed
There was a soul the motions kept;
   But they were all deceived.

For as a watch by art is wound
   To motion, such was mine:
But never had Orinda[1] found
   A soul till she found thine;

Which now inspires, cures and supplies,
   And guides my darkened breast:
For thou art all that I can prize,
   My joy, my life, my rest.

No bridegroom's nor crown-conqueror's mirth
   To mine compared can be:
They have but pieces of this earth,
   I've all the world in thee.

Then let our flame still light and shine
   And no false fear control,
As innocent as our design,
   Immortal as our soul.

---

[1] **Orinda**  Katherine Philips herself

# Mary Sidney, Countess of Pembroke (1561–1621)

Mary Sidney completed the translation of the Psalms begun by her brother, Philip. Both the themes of the Psalms and the style in which they were translated can be seen to influence subsequent religious poetry.

### Excerpts from Translation of 'Psalm 57'

Thy mercy Lord, Lord now thy mercy show,
        On thee I lie,
        To thee I fly,
   Hide me, hive me[1] as thine own
   Till these blasts be overblown,
Which now do fiercely blow.
...

My soul encagèd lies with lions' brood,
       Villains whose hands
       Are fiery brands[2],
  Teeth more sharp than shaft or spear,
  Tongues far better edge do bear
Than swords to shed my blood.
...

Me to entangle every way I go,
       Their trap and net
       Is ready set.
  Holes they dig, but their own holes
  Pitfalls make for their own souls:
So, Lord, oh serve them so.

My heart prepared, preparèd is my heart,
       To spread thy praise
       With tunèd lays[3]:
 Wake my tongue, my lute awake,
 Thou my harp the consort make,
My self will bear a part[4].
...

Myself when first the morning shall appear,
       With voice and string
       So will thee sing[5],
 That this earthly globe, and all
 Treading on this earthly ball,
My praising notes shall hear.
...

As high as highest heaven can give thee place,
    Oh Lord ascend,
    And thence extend
With most bright, most glorious show,
Over all the earth below,
The sunbeams of thy face.

---

[1] **hive me**  shelter me like a bee in a hive
[2] **fiery brands**  burning torches
[3] **lays**  songs
[4] **bear a part**  take part; play one line of the harmony
[5] **So will thee sing**  will sing of you in such a way

---

# Sir Philip Sidney (1554–1586)

### Translation of 'Psalm 13'

How long, O Lord, shall I forgotten be?
    What? Ever?
How long wilt thou thy hidden face from me
    Dissever[1]?

How long shall I consult with careful sprite[2]
    In anguish?
How long shall I with foes' triumphant might
    Thus languish?

Behold me, Lord, let to thy hearing creep
    My crying;
Nay give me eyes, and light, lest that I sleep
    In dying;

Lest my foe brag, that in my ruin he
    Prevailèd,
And at my fall they joy that, troublous, me
    Assailèd.

No, no, I trust on thee, and joy in[3] thy
    Great pity.
Still therefore of thy graces shall be my
    Song's ditty.

METAPHYSICAL POETRY

³**joy in**  rejoice in

# Henry Vaughan (1621–1695)

### 'The Night'

*John* iii, 2

> Through that pure virgin-shrine¹,
> That sacred veil drawn o'er thy glorious noon
> That men might look and live as glow-worms shine,
> And face the moon,
> Wise Nicodemus saw such light
> As made him know his God by night.
>
> Most blest believer he!
> Who in that land of darkness and blind eyes
> Thy long expected healing wings could see,
> When thou didst rise,
> And what can never more be done,
> Did at midnight speak with the Sun²!
>
> O who will tell me, where
> He found thee at that dead and silent hour!
> What hallowed solitary ground did bear
> So rare a flower,
> Within whose sacred leaves did lie
> The fullness of the Deity³.
>
> No mercy-seat of gold,
> No dead and dusty cherub, nor carved stone,
> But his own living works did my Lord hold
> And lodge alone;
> Where trees and herbs did watch and peep
> And wonder, while the Jews did sleep.

Dear night! This world's defeat;
The stop to busy fools; care's check and curb;
The day of spirits; my soul's calm retreat
    Which none disturb!
Christ's progress, and his prayer time;
The hours to which high Heaven doth chime.

God's silent, searching flight:
When my Lord's head is filled with dew⁴, and all
His locks are wet with the clear drops of night;
    His still, soft call;
His knocking time⁵; the soul's dumb watch,
When spirits their fair kindred catch⁶.

Were all my loud, evil days
Calm and unhaunted as is thy dark tent⁷,
Whose peace but by some angel's wing or voice
    Is seldom rent⁸;
Then I in Heaven all the long year
Would keep, and never wander here.

But living where the sun
Doth all things wake, and where all mix and tire
Themselves and others, I consent and run
    To every mire⁹,
And by this world's ill-guiding light,
Err¹⁰ more than I can do by night.

There is in God (some say)
A deep, but dazzling darkness; as men here
Say it is late and dusky, because they
    See not all clear;
O for that night! Where I in him
Might live invisible and dim.

---

¹ **virgin-shrine/That sacred veil**  Christ's
  human body; the 'veil' of his body is like
  the night veiling the sun
² **the Sun**  Christ, both 'Sun' and Son of God
³ **The fullness of the Deity**  the
  completeness of the Godhead
⁴ **my Lord's head is filled with dew**  Christ
  would pray at night

⁵ **His knocking time**  Christ knocks at the
  door willing to enter
⁶ **When spirits … catch**  when souls think
  about relatives who have died
⁷ **thy dark tent**  the night sky
⁸ **rent**  torn
⁹ **mire**  the 'muddiness' of day-to-day living
¹⁰ **Err**  wander off course; sin

METAPHYSICAL POETRY

### 'They Are All Gone into the World of Light!'

They are all gone into the world of light![1]
   And I alone sit lingering here;
Their very memory is fair and bright,
     And my sad thoughts doth clear.

It glows and glitters in my cloudy breast
   Like stars upon some gloomy grove,
Or those faint beams in which this hill is dressed,
     After the sun's remove.

I see them walking in an air of glory,
   Whose light doth trample[2] on my days:
My days, which are at best but dull and hoary,
     Mere glimmering and decays.

O holy hope! and high humility,
   High as the Heavens above!
These are your walks, and you have showed them me
     To kindle my cold love,

Dear, beauteous death! the jewel of the just,
   Shining nowhere, but in the dark;
What mysteries do lie beyond thy dust;
     Could man outlook that mark[3]!

He that hath found some fledged bird's nest, may know
   At first sight, if the bird be flown;
But what fair well, or grove he sings in now,
     That is to him unknown.

And yet, as Angels in some brighter dreams
   Call to the soul, when man doth sleep:
So some strange thoughts transcend our wonted themes[4],
     And into glory peep.

If a star were confined into a tomb
   Her captive flames must needs burn there;
But when the hand that locked her up, gives room,
     She'll shine through all the sphere.

O Father of eternal life, and all
    Created glories under thee!
Resume thy spirit from this world of thrall
        Into true liberty[5].

Either disperse these mists, which blot and fill
    My perspective[6] (still) as they pass,
Or else remove me hence unto that hill[7],
        Where I shall need no glass[8].

---

[1] **They are all gone into the world of
    light!** those who have died before him
    are in heaven
[2] **trample** not unkindly, but because it is far
    brighter
[3] **outlook that mark** look beyond the 'dust'
    of death
[4] **transcend our wonted themes** go
    beyond our normal subjects

[5] **Resume thy spirit from this world of
    thrall / Into true liberty** take back my
    spirit (which belongs to you) from the
    world of slavery in the body into true
    liberty
[6] **perspective** telescope
[7] **that hill** heaven
[8] **glass** telescope

---

# Sir Henry Wotton (1568–1639)

Henry Wotton was a friend of Donne and the recipient of some of his verse letters.
The poem below illustrates the confidence of a Protestant who believes himself to
be saved; many of Donne's sonnets reveal a much greater uncertainty. In the
second verse Wotton says that Christ's death on the cross has ensured that he will
be saved without any need for the Roman Catholic aids of extreme unction (being
anointed with oil by a priest before death), the rosary (an aid to saying prayers in a
particular order), praying to the saints or being purified by the fires of Purgatory.

### 'A Hymn to my God in a Night of my Late Sickness'

Oh thou great power, in whom I move,
For whom I live, to whom I die,
Behold me through thy beams of love,
Whilst on this couch of tears I lie;
    And cleanse my sordid soul within,
    By thy Christ's blood, the bath of sin[1].

No hallowed oils, no grains[2] I need,
No rags of saints, no purging fire,
One rosy drop from David's Seed[3]
Was worlds of seas, to quench thine ire[4].
    Oh precious ransom! which once paid,
    That *Consummatum Est*[5] was said:

And said by him, that said no more,
But sealed it with his sacred breath.
Thou then, that hast disponged my score[6],
And dying, wast the death of death;
    Be to me now, on thee I call,
    My Life, my Strength, my Joy, my All.

---

[1] **the bath of sin** Christ's blood washes
    away sin
[2] **grains** beads of a rosary
[3] **rosy drop from David's Seed** drop of
    blood from David's descendant, Christ
[4] **ire** anger

[5] ***Consummatum Est*** Christ's words on
    the cross: 'It is finished.'
[6] **disponged my score** wiped out what I
    owe for my sins

---

# Lady Mary Wroth (1587–c 1653)

## Song: 'Sweetest Love Return Again'

Sweetest love return again,
    Make not too long stay
Killing mirth and forcing pain,
    Sorrow leading way:
Let us not thus parted be,
Love and absence ne'er agree.

But since you must needs depart,
    And me hapless[1] leave,
In your journey take my heart,
    Which will not deceive:
Yours it is, to you it flies,
Joying in those lovèd eyes.

So in part we shall not part,
    Though we absent be;
Time nor place nor greatest smart
    Shall my bands[2] make free:
Tied I am, yet think it gain;
In such knots I feel no pain.

But can I live, having lost
    Chiefest part of me?
Heart is fled, and sight is crossed[3]:
    These my fortunes be.
Yet dear heart go, soon return:
As good there, as here to burn[4].

---

[1] **hapless**  unlucky
[2] **bands**  fetters
[3] **crossed**  blocked

[4] **there, as here to burn**  to burn with love
or grief in her beloved's breast when he
is away, as when he is with her

---

## 'Good Now, Be Still, and Do Not Me Torment'

Good now, be still, and do not me torment
    With multitudes of questions, be at rest,
    And only let me quarrel with my breast,
    Which still lets in new storms my soul to rent[1].
Fie, will you still my mischiefs more augment?
    You say I answer cross[2], I that confessed
    Long since; yet must I ever be oppressed
    With your tongue torture which will ne'er be spent[3]?
Well then, I see no way but this will fright
    That devil speech: Alas, I am possessed[4],
    And mad folks senseless are of wisdom's right;
The hellish spirit, Absence, doth arrest
    All my poor senses to his cruel might:
    Spare me then till I am myself, and blest.

---

[1] **rent**  rend; tear
[2] **answer cross**  deliberately misinterpreting
    the question

[3] **ne'er be spent**  never be finished
[4] **possessed**  possessed by a devil and
    therefore mad

# John Evelyn (1620–1706)

### *Extract from his* Diary *for Christmas Day 1657*

I went to London with my wife, to celebrate Christmas-day, Mr. Gunning preaching in Exeter chapel ... as he was giving us the Holy Sacrament[1], the chapel was surrounded with soldiers, and all the communicants and assembly surprised and kept prisoners by them, some in the house, others carried away. It fell to my share to be confined to a room in the house, where yet I was permitted to dine with the master of it, the Countess of Dorset, Lady Hatton, and some others of quality who invited me. In the afternoon came Col. Whaly, Goffe and others, from Whitehall, to examine us one by one ... When I came before them they took my name and abode, examined me why, contrary to an ordinance made that none should any longer observe the superstitious time of the Nativity (so esteemed by them), I durst offend, and particularly be at Common Prayers, which they told me was but the mass in English, and particularly pray for Charles Stuart, for which we had no Scripture. I told them that we did not pray for Cha. Stuart, but for all Christian Kings, Princes, and Governors. They replied, in so doing we prayed for the K. of Spain too, who was their enemy and a papist[2], with other frivolous and ensnaring questions and much threatening; and finding no colour[3] to detain me, they dismissed me with much pity of my ignorance. These were men of high flight and above ordinances, and spake spiteful things of our Lord's Nativity. As we went up to receive the Sacrament the miscreants held their muskets against us as if they would have shot us at the altar, but yet suffering[4] us to finish the office of Communion, as perhaps not having instructions what to do in case they found us in that action. So I got home late the next day, blessed be God.

---

[1] **Holy Sacrament** the consecrated bread and wine of the Holy Communion service

[2] **papist** Roman Catholic

[3] **colour** excuse

[4] **suffering** allowing

# 4 | Critical approaches to the poetry

- What have critics seen as the principal strengths and weaknesses of the metaphysical poets?

- How can differing critical approaches increase your understanding and enjoyment of the poems?

The history of changing critical responses to the metaphysical poets reflects changing cultural values and concerns, but also provides a reminder that there are more ways of studying a poet than those fashionable at any particular time.

## Early views

The judgement of Donne's exact contemporary, the playwright and poet Ben Jonson, combines admiration with an awareness of those aspects of Donne's style that would later make him fall out of favour. In conversation with the Scottish poet William Drummond in 1619, Jonson describes Donne as 'the first poet in the world for some things', but he also comments that 'Donne, for not keeping of accent [making his poems scan rhythmically], deserved hanging' and that 'Donne himself, for not being understood, would perish'.

Thomas Carew in his 'Elegy upon the Death of Doctor Donne, Dean of Paul's', published with the posthumous collection of Donne's poetry in 1633, takes up the same issues of Donne's wit and rugged versification both by comment and imitation (try saying aloud the third line quoted here), but sees them as virtues (lines 49–52):

> Since to the awe of thy imperious wit
> Our troublesome language bends, made only fit
> With her tough thick-ribbed hoops, to gird about
> Thy giant fancy ...

By the end of the 17th century Jonson's judgement appeared to be justified, when Dryden dismissively observed that Donne 'affects the metaphysics [makes a show of being philosophical]' in his love poetry and 'perplexes the minds of the fair sex with nice [subtle] speculations of philosophy, when he should engage their hearts, and entertain them with the softnesses of love'. Although his love poetry was dismissed for its difficulty, his wit in satirical matters continued to be admired, even if the style in which it was expressed was felt to be clumsy. Dryden asked, 'Would not Donne's Satires, which abound with so much wit, appear more charming if he had taken care of his words, and of his numbers [his **scansion**]?'

Alexander Pope (1688–1744) acted upon this suggestion in his 'Satires of Dr. John Donne, Dean of St. Paul's Versified', rewriting in much more regular verse the second and fourth satires and updating their attacks on uninspired poets, unscrupulous lawyers and dubious hangers-on at court.

Pope was more critical of Crashaw, of all the metaphysicals perhaps the most different in style from Donne, finding in his work only 'pretty conceptions, fine metaphors, glittering expressions, and something of a neat cast of verse'. Nevertheless, Pope is generally agreed to have made some unacknowledged borrowings from Crashaw in his own poetry. Interestingly, Pope ranked Crashaw above Herbert, a view contrary to most recent opinion, but one which has always had its supporters.

Marvell's poetry was disregarded in the 18th century. Instead, he was honoured as a satirist and political thinker, the writer of prose works which were seen as a patriotic defence of democracy against high-handed, autocratic government.

## Samuel Johnson's criticism of metaphysical poetry

When Samuel Johnson wrote his *Lives of the Poets* in the late 18th century, he took up Dryden's expression and wrote of 'a race of writers that may be termed metaphysical poets'. However, his life of Cowley was the only one of the 56 short biographies to deal with a 'metaphysical' poet, and when he made his analysis of the metaphysical style the only poets he quoted besides Cowley were Donne and Cleveland. There was no mention of George Herbert, whose piety might have been expected to appeal to the deeply religious Johnson, nor of Marvell or Crashaw. Johnson was familiar, however, with the works of both Crashaw and Herbert, quoting them in his dictionary 103 and 78 times respectively. His singling out of Cowley – whose poetry in any case he criticised strongly – seems strange to modern tastes, since Cowley's witty conceits are often thought to be ornamental rather than typically metaphysical 'instruments of definition in an argument or instruments to persuade', as the critic Helen Gardner put it in her attempt to pin down what makes a poem 'metaphysical' (see pages 106–107).

Like Dryden and Pope, Johnson criticised the metaphysical style both for the rugged, naturalistic movement of its verse and for what he saw as the perversely outlandish nature of its imagery:

> The metaphysical poets were men of learning, and to show their learning was their whole endeavour; but, unluckily resolving to show it in rhyme, instead of writing poetry they only wrote verses, and very often such verses as stood the trial of the finger better than of the ear; for the modulation was so imperfect, that they were only found to be verses by counting the syllables. ...

... wit ... may be ... considered as a kind of *discordia concors;* a combination of dissimilar images, or discovery of occult [hidden] resemblances in things apparently unlike. Of wit, thus defined, they have more than enough. The most heterogeneous [completely unrelated] ideas are yoked [joined] by violence together; nature and art are ransacked for illustrations, comparisons, and allusions. ...

Their attempts were always analytic; they broke every image into fragments; and could no more represent, by their slender [insignificant] conceits and laboured particularities [specific details to which too much time has been devoted], the prospects of nature, or the scenes of life, than he who dissects a sunbeam with a prism can exhibit the wide effulgence [brilliance] of a summer noon. ...

Yet great labour, directed by great abilities, is never wholly lost: if they frequently threw away their wit upon false conceits, they likewise sometimes struck out unexpected truth; if their conceits were far-fetched, they were often worth the carriage [cost of transport; in other words the effort that went into them]. To write on their plan, it was at least necessary to read and think.

## Romantic criticism: Coleridge and 19th-century views

Although Donne's style is very far from that of the Romantic poets, it is he in particular who remains an object of interest in the early 19th century. Samuel Taylor Coleridge (1772–1834), poet, critic and philosopher, was clearly fascinated by just those qualities that Carew praised. He showed a sensitive alertness to the rhythmical challenges that had troubled readers from Dryden to Johnson, as well as an appreciation of Donne's wit:

To read Dryden, Pope, etc., you need only count syllables; but to read Donne you must measure Time, and discover the Time of each word by the sense of Passion.

Wonder-exciting vigour, intenseness and peculiarity of thought, using at will the almost boundless stores of a capacious memory, and exercised on subjects where we have no right to expect it – this is the wit of Donne!

Coleridge's enthusiasm is summed up in these lines from *Literary Remains* (1836):

With Donne, whose muse on dromedary trots,
Wreathe iron pokers into true-love knots;
Rhyme's sturdy cripple, fancy's maze and clue,
Wit's forge and fire-blast, meaning's press and screw.

Coleridge also read Herbert, whose poems had been as unfashionable as his approach to religion during the 18th century. He gradually came to value Herbert for a style in which 'the scholar and the poet supplies the material, but the perfect well-bred gentleman the expression and the arrangement'. Such a view of Herbert explains why he continued to remain unfashionable in the Romantic period, although some of his poems were sung as hymns.

Coleridge also praised Crashaw's 'power and opulence of invention', and said that he had had lines from 'A Hymn to St Teresa' in mind when composing the second part of 'Christabel' (a verse tale of the supernatural) in 1800. He did, however, wish that Crashaw had been more willing to prune his work in revision.

Coleridge's opinions were not typical. The general difficulty that the Romantics had with the metrical irregularity and ingenious conceits of metaphysical poetry is made clear when Coleridge's contemporary, the essayist and critic William Hazlitt (1778-1830), wrote of Donne in 1819 that he was 'led, particularly in his satires, to tell disagreeable truths in as disagreeable a way as possible, or to convey a pleasing and affecting thought (of which there are many to be found in his other writings) by the harshest means, and with the most painful effort'. Hazlitt had still less time for Crashaw's 'opulence of invention', saying that Crashaw wrote as he did because he had been 'converted from Protestantism to Popery (a weakness to which the "seething brains" of the poets in this period were prone)'.

Marvell, who had remained well known for his political writings, attracted favourable attention from Edgar Allan Poe (1809–1849), the American poet, writer and critic. What Poe valued in the poetry was its Romantic quality, rather than the irony that was later to be praised. In writing about 'The Nymph Complaining for the Death of her Fawn', he praises 'the sweet melody of the words' and says that the poem 'is positively crowded with nature and with pathos [pity and sadness]'. The English poet Tennyson (1807–1898) also approved the pathos of Marvell's verse, reciting 'To His Coy Mistress' and 'dwelling ... on the magnificent hyperbole, the powerful union of pathos and humour', a reaction that you may wish to compare with the very different one of Francis Barker given below.

## Early 20th-century approaches

The revival of interest in metaphysical poetry at the end of the 19th century culminated in the publication of Herbert Grierson's anthology, *Metaphysical Lyrics and Poems of the Seventeenth Century,* in 1921 and in T.S. Eliot's influential essay 'The Metaphysical Poets', published in the same year. Grierson's anthology helped to establish which 17th-century poets were thought of as typically 'metaphysical'. It also put the emphasis on the shorter poems (doubtless partly because of the constraints of space in an anthology) and in particular on those dealing with love and religion. Eliot's essay did much to create what became the orthodox view of the metaphysicals for 50 years, despite the fact that on one key assertion – that the metaphysical style combined thought and feeling – Eliot was later to change his mind.

Eliot points out how difficult it is to find 'any precise use of metaphor, simile, or other conceit, which is common to all the poets and at the same time important enough … to isolate these poets as a group'. He then refers to the metaphysical conceit, such as the compasses image in 'A Valediction: Forbidding Mourning' ('the elaboration … of a figure of speech to the furthest stage to which ingenuity can carry it'), but goes on to contrast this with 'a development by rapid association of thought which requires considerable agility on the part of the reader'. He quotes a stanza from 'A Valediction: of Weeping' that Johnson had used to illustrate the far-fetched nature of metaphysical imagery:

> On a round ball
> A workman that hath copies by, can lay
> An Europe, Afrique, and an Asia,
> And quickly make that, which was nothing, All,
>> So doth each tear,
>> Which thee doth wear,
> A globe, yea world by that impression grow,
> Till thy tears mixed with mine do overflow
> This world, by waters sent from thee, my heaven dissolvèd so.

**ball** globe
**lay** paste
**Which thee doth wear** which carries your image as a reflection
**impression** reflection

Here we find at least two connexions which are not implicit in the first figure [of speech], but are forced upon it by the poet: from geographer's globe to the tear, and the tear to the deluge [the Flood].

Eliot then quotes Samuel Johnson ('the most heterogeneous ideas are yoked by violence together'), but goes on to argue that 'a degree of heterogeneity of material compelled into unity by the operation of the poet's mind is omnipresent in poetry': in other words, in all poetry you can find elements that are quite unrelated, but which are combined by the power of the poet's thought and imagination.

What Eliot admires in Donne's poetry is 'a direct sensuous apprehension of thought [a grasping of ideas directly through the senses / as directly as the senses respond to stimuli], or a re-creation of thought into feeling'. The difficulty of the metaphysicals was, he argues, because they 'were trying to find the verbal equivalent for states of mind and feeling'. Eliot's concern is not simply to counter Johnson's powerful arguments about the metaphysicals, but also to make a claim for the kind of poetry that he was writing himself: 'it appears likely that poets in our civilisation, as it exists at present [the aftermath of the First World War], must be *difficult*. ... The poet must become more and more comprehensive, more allusive, more indirect, in order to force, to dislocate if necessary, language into his meaning. Hence we get something which looks very much like the conceit ...'.

Eliot's use of a critical essay to advance a theory of poetry which justifies his own approach to writing poetry does not necessarily invalidate what he has to say, but it does remind the student that readings of texts cannot be separated from the circumstances in which they were written.

# Mid 20th-century approaches

## 'New Criticism'

The middle part of the 20th century was dominated by what came to be known as the 'New Criticism'. It was felt that a worthwhile work of literature was complete in itself and could be studied almost independently of its historical background. This 'formalist' approach laid emphasis on such things as the rhythm, syntax and imagery, while looking for such qualities as irony and ambiguity. This approach is conveniently encapsulated in Cleanth Brooks's book *The Well Wrought Urn* (1949), a title taken from Donne's 'The Canonization', in which Donne argues that a brief love poem is as fitting a commemoration of love as something much grander seeming: 'We'll build in sonnets pretty rooms; / As well a well wrought urn becomes / The greatest ashes as half acre tombs'. Brooks writes that 'The Canonization' has its own independence:

> The poem is an instance of the doctrine which it asserts; it is both the assertion and the realisation of the assertion. The poet has actually before our eyes built within the song the 'pretty room' with which he says the lovers can be content. The poem itself is the well-wrought urn ...

Nevertheless, neither Cleanth Brooks nor other 'New Critics' totally ignored the historical background, but for many of them that was exactly what it was, a 'background' that was quite separate from literature. So Brooks can state at the end of an essay written in 1947 on 'An Horatian Ode upon Cromwell's Return from Ireland': 'I have argued that the critic needs the help of the historian – all the help that he can get – but I have insisted that the poem has to be read as a poem – that what it "says" is a question for the critic to answer, and that no amount of historical evidence as such can finally determine what the poem says.'

## *The Metaphysical Poets*: an influential mid-century anthology

In 1957 Penguin Books published *The Metaphysical Poets,* an anthology edited by
Helen Gardner. This took one stage further the recognition that had been begun by
Grierson and Eliot of the metaphysical poets as a group. As well as suggesting poets
for study, it had a short but influential introduction which tackled the issue of what
metaphysical poetry was.

Gardner identified a number of qualities, not all of which she saw as being
exclusive to metaphysical poetry. The first was the quality of being 'strong-lined',
which she described as being the consequence of the 'general desire at the close of
Elizabeth's reign for concise expression, achieved by elliptical syntax [grammatical
omissions], and accompanied by a staccato rhythm in prose and a certain
deliberate roughness in versification in poetry. Along with this went admiration for
difficulty in the thought.' This poetry was not written for publication, but
circulated in manuscript by those whom the professional poet Drayton called
'Chamber poets'. Gardner adds, 'At times the writing has the smell of a **coterie,** the
writer performing with a self-conscious eye on his clever readers. But at its best it
has the ease and artistic sincerity which comes from being able to take for granted
the understanding of the audience for whom one writes.'

In trying to identify this quality more closely, Gardner refers to its
'concentration': 'A metaphysical poem tends to be brief, and is always closely
woven.' This is a quality that she also attributes to Jonson, whom she does not
regard as metaphysical. She links concentration to the popularity of writing
epigrams and comments also on the 'fondness for a line of eight syllables rather
than a line of ten' or for 'stanzas created for the particular poem, in which length of
line and rhyme scheme artfully enforced the sense'.

The second characteristic of metaphysical poetry, which is not shared by
Jonson, is the conceit, which she defines as follows:

> A conceit is a comparison whose ingenuity is more striking than its
> justness, or, at least, is more immediately striking. All comparisons
> discover likeness in things unlike: a comparison becomes a conceit
> when we are made to concede likeness while being strongly
> conscious of unlikeness. A brief comparison can be a conceit if two
> things patently [obviously] unlike, or which we should never think of
> together, are shown to be alike in a single point in such a way, or in
> such a context, that we feel their incongruity.

In addition to the brief conceit which makes a single comparison, Gardner
describes the extended conceit, taking as her example the comparison of a pair of
lovers to the two legs of a compass in 'A Valediction: Forbidding Mourning'. Her

comments on how the conceits work within the poem are worth quoting at some length:

> In a metaphysical poem the conceits are instruments of definition in an argument or instruments to persuade. The poem has something to say which the conceit explicates or something to urge which the conceit helps to forward. It can only do this if it is used with an appearance of logical rigour [strict logic] ... the first impression a conceit makes is of ingenuity rather than justice: the metaphysical conceit aims at making us concede justness [admit appropriateness] while admiring ingenuity.

Gardner then says that the essential quality of a metaphysical poem 'is the vivid imagining of a moment of experience or of a situation out of which the need to argue, or persuade, or define arises'. This is why the poems often have dramatic openings and it is from this that the sense of immediacy arises. She sees the 'strong dramatic imagination of particular situations' as what 'transforms the lyric and makes a metaphysical poem more than an epigram expanded by conceits'. She illustrates this by referring to some of Donne's elegies, including 'To his Mistress Going to Bed'. Interestingly, she makes no comment on the situation from the woman's point of view, but is interested solely in the effect on Donne's style: 'With the tide of passion rising in him, impatient for the moment when she will be his, he watches her undressing for bed. The sense of the moment gives Donne's wit its brilliance and verve, the aptness and incongruity of the comparisons being created by their contexts.'

Not only is Gardner silent on issues that feminists have since taken up; she also values the love poetry without the kind of questioning that it was subsequently to receive:

> The poems which Donne wrote on the experience of loving where love is returned, poems in which 'Thou' and 'I' are merged into 'We', are his most original and profound contributions to the poetry of human love. It is not possible to find models for such poems as 'The Good-Morrow', 'The Anniversarie', 'The Canonization', and, less perfect but still wonderful, 'The Extasie'. These poems have the right to the title metaphysical in its true sense, since they raise, even when they do not explicitly discuss, the great metaphysical question of the relation of the spirit and the senses. They raise it not as an abstract problem, but in the effort to make the experience of the union of human powers in love, and the union of two human beings in love, apprehensible.

Of the religious poetry she says that its strength is that the poets 'bring to their praise and prayer and meditation so much experience that is not in itself religious'.

# Changing critical trends

With an increasing willingness to consider evidence outside the poems themselves, biography came to be seen as an important source of interpretative ideas, although the critic Rosemond Tuve was quick to point out in *A Reading of George Herbert* (1952) that an interpretation of a life based on exclusively modern criteria could be as misleading as an interpretation of the poems without background knowledge:

> Too much has been made of the Herbert who had inner conflicts over giving up the life of the world and the flesh to go into orders [be ordained a priest]; the theme of any symbolic treatment of the love of the soul for Christ ... is the wooing of that soul to gradual submission.

Nevertheless, biography undoubtedly opens up interesting readings, as in John Carey's speculations in *John Donne: Life, Mind, and Art* (1981) about the extent to which Donne's Catholic background may have influenced his poetry. Carey himself, however, points out in his Afterword to the second edition (1990) that the difficulty of dating poems, many of which remained in undated manuscripts for considerable periods of time, has led to interpretations that are over-specific and sometimes highly questionable.

From the 1970s English criticism began to be influenced by a variety of philosophical ideas that led to a questioning of 'common-sense' attitudes to language and historical 'fact'. Literature was no longer seen as a self-contained area separate from other academic subjects such as history, philosophy and psychoanalysis. There was a questioning of the traditional canon, that is the list of poets considered to be worthy of academic study. Women's writing was rediscovered, writing that was not 'high art' began to appear in anthologies, and poets like Crashaw, who had been out of fashion – perhaps because his style had been seen as too foreign and Roman Catholic – were reconsidered.

Some of the more important new approaches are illustrated below. In addition, suggestions for further reading will be found in Part 6: Resources on page 123.

## Making use of the historical and cultural context

Whilst the use of historical evidence to provide a background to the study of literature is not recent, the use of specific items of evidence, sometimes outside the mainstream of traditional historical narrative, is. Poems can also be studied as part of the way in which social and intellectual attitudes and assumptions come to be formed. Thus, in her book, *Heart-Work: George Herbert and the Protestant Ethic* (1999), Cristina Malcolmson quotes the following observation made by George Herbert's elder brother Edward, Lord Herbert of Cherbury:

I do not approve for older brothers that course of study which is ordinary [sic] used in the University, which is, if their parents perchance intend they shall stay there four or five years to employ the said time as if they meant to proceed masters of art and doctors of some science; for which purpose, their tutors commonly spend much time in teaching them subtleties of logic, which as it is usually practised, enables [trains] them for little more than to be excellent wranglers [argumentative debaters], which art, though it may be tolerable in a mercenary lawyer, I can by no means commend in a sober and well-governed gentleman.

Malcolmson goes on to discuss whether George's efforts to purify the style of his religious poems were not only a matter of excluding self-glorification from his poems, but also 'to some extent a means of disavowing or hiding the fervent efforts [of a younger brother] to develop a genteel style and the status such a style could earn'. He had, after all, stayed far more than 'four or five years' at Cambridge and had learnt the 'subtleties of logic' to the point of becoming the university's Public Orator. Malcolmson then invites comparison of the first and fourth verses from 'Perfection' (shown on the left) with the same verses of the poem's later revision, retitled 'The Elixir' (shown on the right):

| Lord teach me to refer | Teach me, my God and King, |
| All things I do to thee | In all things thee to see, |
| That I not only may not err | And what I do in anything, |
| But also pleasing be. | To do it as for thee: |
| | |
| All may of thee partake: | All may of thee partake: |
| Nothing can be so low | Nothing can be so mean, |
| Which with his tincture (for thy sake) | Which with this tincture (for thy sake) |
| Will not to Heaven grow. | Will not grow bright and clean. |

Malcolmson concludes that Herbert's motives for the changes represent a genuinely humble attempt to avoid putting himself forward in his poetry, but adds that the changes he makes here and elsewhere 'also display his anomalous position within the structure of status from the beginning of his career: neither sober gentleman nor mercenary lawyer, neither an established member of the upper classes nor tradesman'.

▶ Compare the two versions for yourself. What evidence can you find to support the claim that Herbert's revision is intended to remove anything that might sound immodest?

An interesting example of how non-literary material can be used to throw light on a text is provided by Francis Barker in his essay 'Into the Vault' on 'To His Coy Mistress' (in *Andrew Marvell*, edited by Thomas Healy, 1998). The starting point is Rembrandt's painting, 'The Anatomy Lesson of Dr Tulp' (1632), in which the body used to illustrate the lesson is laid out in front of the cool gaze of the doctor and those he is teaching. Barker argues that Marvell's poem, in its listing of the parts of the mistress's body to be praised, is a dismemberment comparable to a doctor's dissection of a body. The poem is not a traditional Petrarchan blazon (itemising) of the beloved's beauty (see page 44), but is halfway between the clinical detachment of the new scientific approach pictured by Rembrandt and the earlier savage attitude to the body revealed in the dismemberment of those condemned to death and in the spectacularly gruesome scenes of Jacobean tragedy, such as the entry of Giovanni in Ford's *'Tis Pity She's a Whore* with his sister's heart on the point of his dagger:

> So that as that last cut which 'should show your Heart' offers to the enquiring gaze of the surgeons gathered round the table the chief of the vital organs, so it also displays that bloody pumping heart which was so often held aloft to one audience or another gathered at the foot of the public scaffold, dramatic [theatre stage] or penal [place of execution]. ... [the readers are] spectators where the lover's caress turns into an act of Jacobean slaughter and where the king's wrath issues in corporal revenge.

Barker goes on to argue that the alleged savagery of this 'dismemberment' prepares the way for the threat of death as a means of forcing the woman to accept the man's desires:

> Behind the initial banter of the lover's discourse and its ingenious persuasiveness is the implacable rattle of 'Time's winged Charriot hurrying near', in the path of which what the male *persona* soon perceives in the woman's 'coy' reluctance as an artful refusal of sexuality comes to look more like a stubborn and destructive wilfulness, and her silence ... sullen denial ... After all, Time is bearing down, and with it the entire weight and fury of the patriarchal tradition which, in the real republic [public world], however much its ideology may mark out chastity as a proper register of femininity [acceptable mode of feminine behaviour], none the less exists to secure the subordination of women.

# Gender and feminist approaches

The partial account given above of Barker's essay on 'To His Coy Mistress' also serves to illustrate how a cultural approach can raise gender issues. The very fact that the woman is silent in this poem, as also in so many of Donne's love poems, raises questions about how the poems should be read. One question in particular is whether these are poems of manipulation, imposing masculine values in order to dominate and control. This is an issue that is related to social and historical considerations both because of women's place in society (for example, their lack of property rights in marriage and the importance of chastity – see page 50) and also because of the frequency with which male possession of a woman is likened to colonisation or capturing booty.

A feminist approach would question whether writing such as this – like Donne's claim that his mistress is 'both the Indias of spice and mine' in 'The Sun Rising' – is truly complimentary or merely reveals a masculine assumption that women are like precious commodities that can be captured and traded.

Feminist criticism also studies women's writing of the period, both in its own right and also to throw light on men's writing. It is revealing, for example, to look at how Philips adapts Donne's images, as she does on a number of occasions, to express a woman's point of view. For example, in 'Friendship's Mysteries, To my Dearest Lucasia' (Part 3, pages 88–89) Donne's line: 'She is all states, and all princes, I', is rephrased as a statement of mutual love:

> Divided joys are tedious found,
>   And griefs united easier grow:
> We are ourselves but by rebound,
>   And all our titles shuffled so,
> Both princes, and both subjects too.

In a similar way Philips reworks the compasses image from 'A Valediction: Forbidding Mourning' (Part 3, page 70) in these lines 21–36 from 'Friendship in Emblem':

> The compasses that stand above
> Express this great immortal love;
> For friends, like them, can prove this true:
> They are, and yet they are not, two;
>
> And in their posture is expressed
> Friendship's exalted interest:
> Each follows where the other leans,
> And what each does, the other means.

And as when one foot does stand fast,
And t'other circles seeks to cast,
The steady part does regulate
And make the wanderer's motion straight,

So friends are only two in this,
To reclaim each other when they miss:
For whosoe'er will grossly fall,
Can never be a friend at all.

▶ How has Philips altered the image of the compasses to stress the equality of the relationship that she describes? How does a comparison of the poems affect your response both to them and to other love poetry of the period?

*Poor Petrarch - much copied but some beautiful moments!*

One claim that Donne makes in justifying his rejection of Petrarchan poetry is that 'Love's not so pure, and abstract, as they use [are accustomed] / To say, which have no mistress but their Muse [goddess of poetic inspiration]' ('Love's Growth'). In other words, he argues that this kind of poetry is written as a poetic exercise and is not based on a relationship with an actual woman. However, a question that gender criticism raises is how far the love poetry of Donne is written for women at all, or whether it is really written for other male members of his coterie. That certainly seems to have been the view of Margaret Cavendish, Duchess of Newcastle (1623–1673). In this extract from 'The Clasp' (lines 5–8), she was clear that poetry should be derived from 'Nature' and not the 'Art' of the 'Pedant', in other words, the unnatural contrivances of writers obsessed with displaying learning:

Give me a style that Nature frames, not Art;
For Art doth seem to take the Pedant's part.
And that seems noble, which is easy, free,
Not to be bound with o're-nice pedantry.

**frames** constructs
**o're-nice** fussily precise

Consequently she is dismissive of much men's poetry, writing in 1655: 'The reason why men run in such obscure conceits, is because they think their wit will be esteemed ... as if to express a thing hard, were to make it better'. If she is right, then far from 'perplexing the minds of the fair sex' with his conceits, as Dryden thought, Donne had an entirely different audience in mind as he wrote: the male coterie amongst whom copies of his poems were circulated.

One way of reading the poems which assumes that they are not addressed to particular women is given opposite. It is based on what is claimed to be evidence within the poems themselves of the improbability of the love described.

*but maybe*

# Deconstruction

Deconstruction is a relatively recent approach that involves searching for and bringing out the hidden and conflicting aspects of a text, and finding new readings by studying the gap between what language appears to be asserting and the things that it is perhaps denying or hiding. Like the other approaches already discussed, this one is not necessarily followed in isolation. Barker's essay on 'To His Coy Mistress', to which reference has already been made to illustrate cultural and gender approaches, can be seen as using these approaches in a typically deconstructive manner to destabilise a traditional reading of the poem.

In her article 'Songs and Sonets as Self-Consuming Artifact' (*Donne*, New Casebooks, 1999), Tilottama Rajan also follows a deconstructive approach, arguing that Donne's love poems have a rhetoric which 'seems to be self-authenticating [establishing its own genuineness] but turns out, on closer inspection, to call attention to the insufficiency of its own procedures'. She points out that this approach is justified not simply by modern critical theory, but by the fact that Renaissance sonnet sequences such as Sidney's and Shakespeare's are 'not only the story of an emotional relationship, but also the narrative of their own construction [description of how they were written]' – as in the opening sonnet of Sidney's *Astrophel and Stella* when at the end of a discussion as to how love can be described he finishes: 'Fool, said my muse to me, look in thy heart and write.'

The far-fetched nature of the compasses conceit in 'A Valediction: Forbidding Mourning', for example, alerts the reader to the fact that the claim that the lovers will remain united 'is based on a poetic fiction, on invention rather than logic'. *–really?* Similarly the witty argument of 'The Sun Rising' 'asks to be resisted'. The sun, after all, is only eclipsed by the lover shutting his eyes and refusing to accept the truth. Even the final hyperbole claiming that the lovers in their bed represent the whole world and that the sun can do its duty by warming them alone is arguably undermined by being based on the old-fashioned idea that the sun goes round the world rather than vice-versa. *or simply at as accepted*

At the end of the article, Rajan observes that many Renaissance sonnet sequences claim that the beloved's beauty will be preserved for ever in their poetry, as in this example from Shakespeare's Sonnet 55:

> Not marble, nor the gilded monuments
> Of princes, shall outlive this powerful rhyme,
> But you shall shine more bright in these contents
> Than unswept stone, besmeared with sluttish time.

*no more 'false' than*
*Death Thou shalt die*
*really – its a*
*matter of argument*
*– how its accepted*
*can be 'light' or 'heavy'*

She finds no such assertion in Donne's love poems and suggests that his underlying attitude is critical of the exaggerated claims of unchanging love made by earlier poets and is much better indicated by this quotation from his 'Second Anniversary': 'whilst you think you be / Constant, you are hourly in inconstancy'.

Readings like this are based on the assumption that meaning is not a 'given' (an already established and unchanging truth) that you will find embodied in the words of the text if you search long enough. Rather, meaning is dependent on changing historical and cultural contexts: it was not absolute in the past, nor is it now. At first sight, such a view is rather worrying – what is the point of trying to work out any meaning at all? – but it is also liberating and encourages the adventurous reader to balance a variety of possible readings and enjoy a richer response to the poetry.

Yes – but surely requires careful handling by students at the mercy of examiners who may – or may not – be open minded.

## Assignments

1 'The most heterogeneous ideas are yoked by violence together.' (Samuel Johnson, 1778)

'When a poet's mind is perfectly equipped for its work it is constantly amalgamating disparate experience.' (T.S. Eliot, 1921)

'… the first impression a conceit makes is of ingenuity rather than justice: the metaphysical conceit aims at making us concede justness while admiring ingenuity …' (Helen Gardner, 1957)

Analyse three or four metaphysical poems in detail to show which of these judgements you agree with. Is the way that the imagery functions a major issue in the poems you have chosen, or do they depend for their impact on other things?

2 Read 'To my Excellent Lucasia, on our Friendship' (Part 3, page 90) in which Katherine Philips writes: 'No bridegroom's nor crown-conqueror's mirth / To mine compared can be,' when talking of her friendship. Does a married woman's claim to find more happiness in female friendship than a husband can at his wedding add to the weight of Barker's argument about 'To His Coy Mistress'?

3 In what ways does an awareness that Donne may have had a male coterie of fellow writers and wits in mind when he wrote his love poetry affect your reading of it? How valid do you find Helen Gardner's comment about 'the ease and artistic sincerity which comes from being able to take for granted the understanding of the audience for whom one writes' (page 106)?

# How to write about metaphysical poetry

## The initial approach: close reading

For an illustration of some of the aspects you might wish to consider when first reading a poem, see the beginning of Part 2: Approaching the poems on page 39.

Initial questions that you might ask on reading a poem could be:

- What is this poem about?
- What techniques has the poet used to express thought and feeling?

You will need to consider what such features as rhyme, rhythm and pattern contribute to a poem's effect. Do they, for example, reinforce the sense of a natural spoken voice, suggest particular emotions or reflect the complexity of a line of reasoning?

Does the choice of verse form help to reflect the ideas expressed in it? You might look, for example, at the use Donne makes of the way the rhyme pattern of his sonnets breaks them up into three quatrains (groups of four lines) and a rhyming couplet at the end, or the use Herbert makes of the short line at the end of each verse in 'Virtue'. Comparison of the many varieties of verse form used either by a single poet or by different poets is a valuable way of bringing out the distinctive qualities of a particular form.

Other features that you will need to consider have more to do with the nature of the poets' ideas than with the outward form in which they are expressed. Paradox, for example, is found in the complexities of love (in Donne's 'To Let Me Live, Oh Love and Hate Me too'; 'The Prohibition', line 24), as well as in such religious ideas as that to serve God is freedom (the end of Donne's 'Batter my Heart') or that death leads to eternal life (in Donne's 'As West and East … are One'; 'Hymn to God my God, in my Sickness', lines 13–14).

Ambiguity may be a means of deliberately leaving the reader different meanings to balance against each other. For example, at the end of Herbert's 'Affliction' ('Let me not love thee, if I love thee not') does 'let' mean 'hinder' or 'allow', or both?

Irony always demands careful attention. In Donne's poem 'The Flea', the reader may assume that it is light-hearted irony when Donne calls his mistress 'cruel and sudden' for killing the flea that he has been using to support his argument, and yet the action of killing the flea is one of the few opportunities that a woman is given within his poems to express an independent opinion. The fact that her action is merely used to open the way for the concluding stage of Donne's argument may lead to a re-appraisal of the irony's function. Marvell's 'An Horatian Ode' opens with the statement that it is time for ambitious young men to abandon 'numbers languishing' (weak, sentimental poetry) and yet, of course, Marvell is writing a poem. Is this an irony that undercuts the poem, or are these 'numbers' not 'languishing', but a legitimate form of action or preparation for action?

# Establishing the context

## The biographical context

Before you are able to answer all the questions raised by an initial close reading, you will need to consider the biographical context:

- For whom was the poem written and when?

- If the poem is in the first person, is the 'speaker' of it the same as the poet?

- Does what you know of the poet's life throw any light on the poem?

It is sometimes easy to find out the first recipient of a poem if it is a letter or carries a dedication, but often it is less obvious. It might be supposed that the love poems were originally intended for the beloved that the poem mentions, but Crashaw's 'Wishes to his (Supposed) Mistress' is a reminder that there is no guarantee that the woman existed in the first place. The writers of other ingenious love poems may often have provided the first audience for a poem. It follows from this that you cannot assume the poems are autobiographical.

While some poems may have been written for a particular coterie of friends and fellow writers, this cannot be taken for granted either. Because so many of the poems were circulated in manuscript, it is hard to be sure when they were written and therefore what the circumstances of composition were. In the case of Marvell, at least one poem that appears to be very public, 'An Horatian Ode', was not in fact published until after his death and does not appear to have been widely circulated either. Many of the poems that were published during his lifetime were published anonymously for political reasons.

▶ The use of biographical detail for the interpretation of individual poems requires caution precisely because of the difficulty of dating the poems, but it is still a valuable approach. What legitimate use can be made of knowledge of the following:

- the career ambitions of Donne and Herbert

- the conversions from and to Roman Catholicism respectively of Donne and Crashaw

- the experiences during the Commonwealth of those poets who were Royalist
- the political career of Marvell?

## The cultural context

In addition to looking at biographical information, you should consider cultural issues:

- How do a poet's ideas and style relate to those of other poets of the time ?
- Does a knowledge of translations of the period help?

Comparison with other poets can be an effective way of highlighting a poet's distinctive qualities. You might, for example, wish to use the extract from Joseph Hall's satire on the 'love-sick poet' published in 1597 (Part 3, page 73) either as evidence of another young man's view of Petrarchan poetry to set alongside Donne's (Hall was two years younger than Donne), or to compare his satirical style with Donne's. You might begin by arguing that what the two writers have in common is a rejection of Petrarchan ideals. This helps to explain why Donne wrote as he did in his more cynical and erotic poems, yet Hall's attitude to women – on the limited evidence here – verges on the misogynistic in a way that Donne's does not. You might of course argue quite the reverse. If you wish to consider satirical style, you might analyse how many of its characteristics are displayed in the work of both writers. In both you might find colloquial language and a willingness to shock. Your attention might also be drawn to certain distinctive qualities of Donne's writing that are less apparent in the extract from Hall: for example, the greater irregularity of Donne's verse which gives a sense of improvisation, the stronger projection of the poet's personality, and a more effective use of wit and irony.

Another way of using comparisons is to pursue a theme, either in a number of contrasting poems by the same poet (Donne's love poems are an obvious example) or in poems by a number of different poets. Thus the issue of the woman's voice, or lack of one, could be discussed by comparing one metaphysical writer with another, perhaps Donne with Marvell; by looking at women writers such as Wroth and Philips; or by comparisons with non-metaphysical poets such as Jonson and Herrick. Needless to say, these approaches can be combined.

You may also find it helpful to look at translations of works that may have influenced the poets, for example, comparing the version of the Psalms by Mary and Philip Sidney with some of Herbert's poetry. Once again it is not simply a matter of finding similarities, but of seeing how ideas and imagery have not only been transferred, but also modified.

# The historical and social context

- Do contemporary religious and political events help to explain the poem?
- Does a knowledge of contemporary social attitudes (for example, towards women) help?

Historical, religious and social knowledge will always be partial and in any case comes as much from the poems you are studying as from other sources. For example, Marvell's poems, prose writings and letters are important sources for the Restoration period. Despite its limitations such knowledge helps in two ways. It provides a background that will prevent you making errors of interpretation based on misunderstandings. It will also help you to appreciate in greater depth how a poet's mind may be working in specific poems. For example, the levelling work of the reapers as they mow the meadow in 'Upon Appleton House' (stanzas 49–53) gains in significance if you are aware of the Parliamentary army's claims to be reapers cutting down the enemies of God. The biblical basis of this claim is found in Isaiah's words 'all flesh is grass' (Chapter 40, verse 6), and the words of the angel in *Revelation* 15 that announce God's vengeance: 'Thrust in thy sickle, and reap'. Awareness of how the Bible was being read politically opens up the possibility of reading subsequent stanzas in 'Upon Appleton House' as a commentary on the Civil Wars.

The concept of 'social attitudes' begs an enormous number of questions. Whose attitudes? Men's or women's? Calvinists' or Catholics'? How can we be sure? Did people change their minds? Are we imposing modern concepts on a period that would not have known what we were talking about? Despite the slipperiness of the idea it is still worthwhile to look at some of the evidence, while bearing in mind that any individual item of evidence may be just that: the opinion of an individual. For example, a diary entry may only represent the feelings of the individual writing it, but it seems reasonable to assume that the extract from John Evelyn's *Diary* for Christmas Day 1657 (Part 3, page 99) tells us something of wider interest about the feelings of supporters of the abolished Church of England under the rule of Cromwell. This in turn can throw light on some of Vaughan's poetry, but can also be contrasted with the attitudes of Marvell in his political poems.

Of particular interest are the attitudes of both sexes when considering the love poetry. What assumptions is Donne making about himself, as well as about his influence on women, when he talks in 'Elegy 16' of 'my words' masculine persuasive force'? Is Marvell making any similar assumptions in 'To His Coy Mistress'? Since presumably both poems are fiction, how seriously should we take what is said anyway? More radically, it has been argued that Donne's aggressive attitude to women in the elegies reflects male resentment of female rule under

Elizabeth I (Achsah Guibbory, 'The Politics of Love in Donne's Elegies' in John *Donne,* New Casebooks, 1999).

The traditional attitude that women were inferior to men and responsible for the Fall was still very much current, but in *Salve Deus Rex Iudaeorum* Aemilia Lanyer cleverly uses Eve's alleged weakness to pass the blame back to Adam (Part 3, page 82). This provides a pointer to the probable feeling of women faced with the traditional accusation of leading men astray, and it could be used as a starting point when writing about a poem of male seduction. The cautious way in which Mary Sidney, Mary Wroth and Katherine Philips approach the publication of their work, and their fears that they will be seen as being too 'forward' in seeking publication, also confirm a prejudice against women in a male-dominated society. Even so, you will still need to beware of making blanket assumptions about the attitudes of all writers, or even about the attitude of a single writer at all times.

## What the critics say

In trying to answer the questions suggested so far, you will need to read other people's responses to the poems. Questions to bear in mind when you do so are:

* Does the critic's interpretation match my own experience when reading the texts?
* In what ways may modern judgements reflect the preoccupations of our own times?
* How have critical judgements changed over the years?

Critics will bring both specialist knowledge (not exclusively literary) and great experience in reading to their interpretations, but you need to remember that they may not necessarily be right! You need to read the poems yourself first and to test your own ideas against what the critics have to say. As you read their opinions, you will find some of your own ideas questioned and others confirmed. You will also soon discover that the critics do not always agree amongst themselves. However, the different insights that they offer into the poems will not necessarily be contradictory, and in combination may give you an even better understanding.

Finally, whatever use you make of the wider contexts in which the poetry was written and of the critical opinions of other people, you must always come back to the poems themselves and use your own judgement to assess the evidence, while keeping an open mind and remembering that, as changing critical opinions have shown, no judgement is likely to be final.

## Assignments

1.  In Carew's elegy, he talks of Donne's 'masculine expression' (Part 3, page 65). Compare some male metaphysical love poetry with the poems of love and friendship written by Mary Wroth and Katherine Philips. Do you find anything distinctively 'masculine' about the metaphysical style?

2.  Show how a knowledge of earlier treatments of a theme has enhanced your understanding of one or more poems. For example, you might consider Donne's reactions to Ovid and Petrarch, the influence of neo-platonic ideas, or why Marvell chose to call his Ode to Cromwell 'Horatian'.

3.  Helen Gardner writes that the strength of the religious poets is that they 'bring to their praise and prayer and meditation so much experience that is not in itself religious'. Compare the way in which any two of the poets you have read write about their relationship with God. What are the predominant images that each poet uses, and what do they suggest to you about the relationship?

4.  Donne, Herbert and Marvell were MPs, Vaughan appears to have fought briefly in the Civil Wars, and Crashaw and Cowley were evicted from their Cambridge fellowships by the Puritans and had to live abroad. Show how your knowledge of the political background of one of these poets has affected your reading of the poetry.

5.  Read the extracts from Mary Sidney's translation of 'Psalm 57' (Part 3, page 91). How does an awareness of the psalm affect your reading of Herbert's description of his troubles in 'Affliction', or of his musical imagery in 'Easter' (pages 74 and 78)?

6.  Write an additional stanza in the style of a poem that you enjoy. Then write a stanza parodying the same poem. What have you learned about the style and technique of the original?

7   Choose four or five poems and prepare them for performance,
    considering how best to place them in relationship to each other in order
    to bring out their meaning. What have you learned about the sound of the
    poems, the 'voices' in which they should be spoken and the ways in
    which their ideas are expressed?

8   Find recordings of some of the musical settings listed in Part 6:
    Resources and listen to them. How suitable do you find the poems as
    lyrics? Is there a noticeable difference in the complexity of ideas and
    irregularity of rhythm in those poems that Donne entitles 'Song' and the
    rest of his poems? In his *Life of Herbert,* Isaak Walton says that Herbert
    'composed many divine hymns and anthems, which he set and sung to
    his lute or viol'. What evidence can you find in Herbert's versification that
    suggests his musical sensitivity?

9   Find illustrations of 16th- and 17th-century emblem books. In what ways
    does the metaphysical conceit go beyond an emblem and its
    accompanying verse?
        Study some baroque paintings of religious subjects: for example,
    Carracci's 'The Virgin Mourning Christ', Rubens' 'Descent of Christ from
    the Cross', Caravaggio's 'Conversion of St Paul', Ribalta's 'Vision of St
    Bernard' or Gaulli's 'The Worship of the Holy Name of Jesus' on the
    ceiling of Il Gesù in Rome.
        Compare the way in which the painters aim to stimulate religious
    devotion with the methods of Crashaw in such poems as 'The Flaming
    Heart'.

# 6 | Resources

## Further reading

### Primary texts

In many cases there are a number of editions to choose from. Those given here have been selected on the grounds of availability, thorough notes and cost, but are by no means the only worthwhile editions.

*Abraham Cowley: Selected Poems,* eds. David Hopkins and Tom Mason (Carcanet, 1994)

*John Donne: The Major Works,* ed. John Carey (Oxford, 1990)
This includes plentiful examples of Donne's prose.

*John Donne: The Complete English Poems,* ed. A.J. Smith (Penguin, 1971)

*George Herbert: The Complete English Poems,* ed. JohnTobin (Penguin, 1991)

*Andrew Marvell: The Complete Poems,* ed. E.S. Donno (Penguin, 1972)

*The Collected Works of Katherine Philips: The Matchless Orinda; Vol 1 The Poems,* ed. Patrick Thomas (Stump Cross Books, 1990)

*Thomas Traherne: Selected Poems and Prose*, ed. Alan Bradford (Penguin, 1991)

*Henry Vaughan: The Complete Poems,* ed. Alan Rudrum (Penguin, 1976)

There is currently no collected edition of Crashaw's poems in print, but there are selections in all the anthologies listed below.

### Anthologies

All of these have introductions, except for the Cummings volume which has a brief introduction for each poet and full annotation. The introduction by Norbrook pays particular attention to the cultural and historical background.

Robert Cummings *Seventeenth-Century Poetry* (Blackwell, 2000)

Helen Gardner *The Metaphysical Poets* (Penguin, 1957, revised 1972)

Germaine Greer, Susan Hastings, Jeslyn Medoff and Melinda Sansone *Kissing the Rod* (Virago, 1988)

David Norbrook and H.R. Woodhuysen *The Penguin Book of Renaissance Verse* (Penguin, 1992)

Marion Wynne-Davies *Women Poets of the Renaissance* (Dent, 1998)

## Criticism
*John Donne: Contemporary Critical Essays,* ed. Andrew Mousley (New Casebooks, Macmillan, 1999)

*Andrew Marvell,* ed. Thomas Healy (Longman, 1998)

*Andrew Marvell,* ed. John Carey (Penguin, 1969)
Still worth reading in its own right and illustrative of earlier critical approaches

Thomas N. Corns, ed. *The Cambridge Companion to English Poetry: Donne to Marvell* (Cambridge, 1993)
A general introduction to the wider poetry of the period with chapters on key themes and on all of the major metaphysicals

David Reid *The Metaphysical Poets* (Longman/Pearson, 2000)
A general introduction with chapters on each of the main metaphysical poets

## Biographies and individual studies
This a very short list with the emphasis primarily on recent studies:

*John Donne: Life, Mind and Art* John Carey (Faber, 1981, revised 1990)

*A Life of George Herbert* Amy Charles (Cornell University Press, 1977)

*World Enough and Time: The Life of Andrew Marvell* Nicholas Murray (Little, Brown, 1999)

*Marvell: The Writer in Public Life* Annabel Patterson (Longman/Pearson, 2000)

*Katherine Philips ('Orinda')* Patrick Thomas (University of Wales Press, 1988)

*Henry Vaughan* Stevie Davies (Poetry Wales Press, 1995)

# Websites

These are plentiful and developing all the time. Amongst the most helpful are:

www.luminarium.org/sevenlit
(also www.luminarium.org/renlit)

Luminarium's two linked sites provide brief biographical details of writers of the late 16th and 17th centuries together with samples of their work and critical essays. There are also sections on History and Politics, Women in Seventeenth-Century England, Renaissance Music, Renaissance Theatre and Art and Architecture .

www.library.utoronto.ca/utel/rp/intro.html

Representative Poetry Online provides examples of poetry by virtually all the writers of the period, together with a timeline and a glossary of critical terms.

www.nationalgallery.org.uk

This is one of a number of museum and gallery sites that will enable you to see examples of paintings of the period.

# Musical recordings

There were two early settings of Donne's 'A Hymn to God the Father'. The first by John Hilton is probably the one that Donne himself took pleasure in hearing sung in St Paul's Cathedral and is on: *Lovesongs and Sonnets of John Donne and Sir Philip Sidney* (Metronome METCD 1006).

The second setting written at the Restoration is by Pelham Humfrey and is on: *Croft – The Burial Service* (earlier issued as *A Solemn Musick*) (EMI CDM 5666832).

There are also several recordings of Britten's 'The Holy Sonnets of John Donne'; try: *Britten Songs* (Hyperion CDA 66823).
This includes a realisation of the Humfrey setting as well.

There are several recordings of Vaughan Williams' settings of five Herbert poems, 'Five Mystical Songs'. One is on *English Vocal Works* (EMI Classics CDM 5655882).

# Glossary

**Allusive**  making references (usually indirectly) to the work of other writers, often by echoing their language, imagery, verse form, etc.

**Analogy**  the use of a similarity to develop a line of reasoning.

**Baroque**  highly elaborate and decorative in style; a term used first of the visual arts and then applied to literature and music as well.

**Calvinist**  following the teaching of the Swiss reformer Calvin, and in particular his doctrine of predestination.

*Carpe diem*  literally: pluck the day (as if it were fruit); a much quoted phrase used by the Roman poet Horace to urge the enjoyment of life while young; it is a common theme of metaphysical love poetry.

**Commonwealth**  not the modern meaning, but the term for the state under the rule of Cromwell after the Civil Wars when England was not a kingdom.

**Conceit**  an ingenious comparison which reveals similarities in things not normally associated with each other.

**Coterie**  a group of people linked by an exclusive interest such as the writing and circulating of poetry.

**Courtly love**  love in which the man idealises and devotedly serves an unobtainable woman.

**Deconstruction**  a form of criticism which explores conflicting meanings within a text.

**Hyperbole**  a figure of speech in which exaggeration is used to emphasise and persuade.

**Irony**  the expression of meaning by words that would suggest the opposite were it not for their context and tone.

**Jesuits**  members of the Society of Jesus founded by St Ignatius Loyola in 1534 to win back Protestants to Roman Catholicism and to do missionary work. Because their first loyalty was to the Roman Catholic Church and not to the excommunicated Elizabeth I (see page 22), they were commonly regarded as traitors.

**Paradox**  a self-contradictory statement that may prove to make sense on closer examination.

**Persona**  the character imagined as the speaker of a poem which is in the first person, but not autobiographical.

**Petrarchan**  using the imagery and ideas associated with the poems of the Italian poet Petrarch (1304–1374).

**Platonic**  literally, associated with the teaching of the Greek philosopher Plato; then associated with love poetry that values spiritual union between lovers to the exclusion of sexual love.

**Predestination**  the belief that God's foreknowledge of everything that is going to happen means that, from the beginning of time, some souls are destined to heaven and some to hell.

**Puritans**  those reformers who wished to 'purify' the English Church further on the grounds that it had not been completely reformed; generally Calvinist in doctrine.

**Scansion**  the rhythmical pattern of poetry.

**Sonnet**  the modern meaning is a 14-line poem either divided into an eight-line and a six-line section (octave and sestet), the Petrarchan sonnet, or into three quatrains and a final rhyming couplet (normally known as a Shakespearean sonnet). Note that it originally meant a short lyrical poem of no particular verse form, as in Donne's *Songs and Sonets*.

**Syntax**  the arrangement of words in a sentence according to grammatical principles.

**Wit**  not humour, but the habit of ingenious thought (for example in the metaphysical conceit).

# Index

Women

Conflict (inner/outer)

Parting / Separation

Faith / Doubt

Devotion

Death / Life & Death / Resurrection

Love ⟨ sexual ⟩ — Both
     ⟨ platonic

Love of God / Love of woman

Discovery / Revelation

Calculation / Analysis

Argument / Proof

    Conceits
    Extended imagery
    Flirtation of love, a mistress
The Global Stage for love — sun          Storm
                           moon
                           stars
                           spheres

Printed in Great Britain
by Amazon.co.uk, Ltd.,
Marston Gate.